P9-BIF-611

CROWSNEST

An Illustrated
History and Guide to
The Crowsnest Pass

May 26, 1996

To Wayne & Penny Whitlock:

J. Brian Dawson

CROWSNEST

An Illustrated History and Guide to The Crowsnest Pass

With Warmest Regards,
Sincerely,
J. Brian Dawson.

Altitude Publishing Canada Ltd.
Canadian Rockies/Vancouver

Dedication

Dedicated, with love, to my wife Patricia,
Jim McIndoe, Doug Graham, and Frank Haika,
all of whom have consistently believed in me;
also, to my dear friends, Rufus and Sabrina,
always there when I need them.

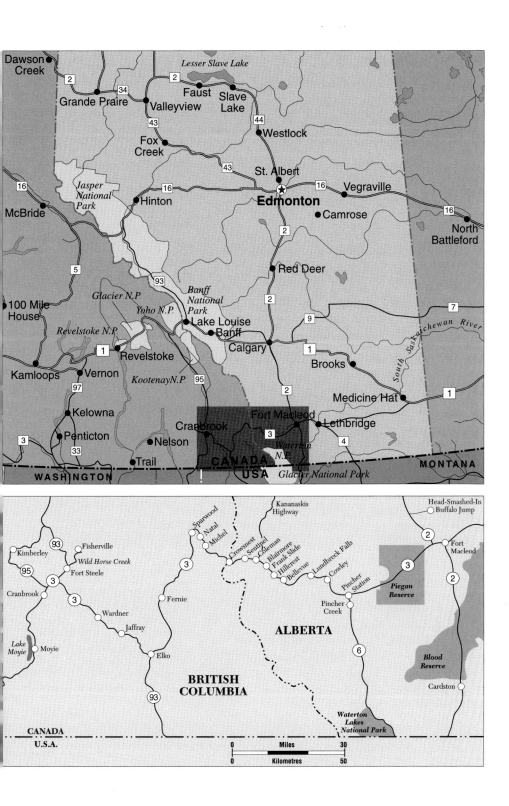

Publishing Information

Copyright 1995 © Altitude
Text Copyright 1995 © J. Brian Dawson
Base Map (page 5) 1994 © Magellan Graphix

All rights reserved. No part of this book may be reproduced in any form or by any means, electronic or mechanical, without prior written permission of the publisher.

Although care has been taken to ensure that all information presented in this book is accurate and up-to-date, neither the author nor the publisher can be held responsible for any errors.

Project Development	Stephen Hutchings
Concept/Art Direction	Stephen Hutchings
Design	Stephen Hutchings
Assistant Designer	Sandra Davis
Editing	Anne Norman
Index/Proofreading	Alison Barr
Maps	Catherine Burgess
	Sandra Davis
FPO Scanning	Debra Symes
Electronic Page Layout	Nancy Green
	Alison Barr
Financial Management	Laurie Smith

Canadian Cataloguing in Publication Data
Dawson, J. Brian (John Brian), 1948-
  Crowsnest
ISBN 1-55153-075-9
1. Crowsnest Pass Region (Alta. and B.C.)--History. I. Title
FC3695.C76D38 1995   971.23'4
  C93-091381-7 F1079.C7D39 1995

Front Cover Photo: Frank Slide Interpretive Centre
Frontispiece: Crowsnest Pass
Back Cover Photo: Leitch Collieries Historic Site

Made in Western Canada
Printed and bound in Canada
by Friesen Printers, Altona, Manitoba.

Altitude GreenTree Program
Altitude Publishing will plant in Western Canada twice as many trees as were used in the manufacturing of this product.

Altitude Publishing Canada Ltd.
1500 Railway Avenue, PO Box 1410
Canmore, Alberta T0L 0M0

Contents

Introduction

I remember very clearly my first impressions of the Crowsnest Pass. When I was a child, my family drove in a car through the area. Seeing the Frank Slide for the first time was something no one would be likely to forget. I remember in particular being amazed at the size of some of the Boulders.

My next personal contact with the Pass came in the early 1980s, when I subcontracted to write a historical report on a church in the district. Then, a couple of years later, I did another such report for the Alberta Historic Sites Service on the Greenhill Hotel in Blairmore. My interest in the history of the Crowsnest Pass was greatly increased by this work. During the course of the latter project, I made a trip to the area for three or four days. The people I met went out of their way to assist me, and I was impressed with their friendliness and courtesy.

The foremost authority on the archeology of the district, Dr. B.O.K. Reeves, has remarked: "The Crowsnest Pass is the most important historic and prehistoric area in the Canadian Rockies. It is of national significance. [In the Rocky Mountains], Crowsnest is the most important valley of all...."[1]

In all respects, the history of the Crowsnest Pass is rich. While the central theme of the past century is coal mining, other concerns also interest one. These run the gamut from prehistoric habitation sites to rum-runners, the Frank Slide, terrible mine disasters, a deadly manhunt after a brazen train robbery, coal miners' strikes, and a lost gold mine—and more. The Guide at the back of the book is invaluable for all visitors to the Crowsnest Pass, including both native Canadians and tourists from other countries.

It is my hope and expectation that you, the reader, will find much of interest in this book. It was a pleasure to compose it, and, I believe, there is something herein for everyone.

J. Brian Dawson

Chapter 1
The Pass Takes Shape

About 100 million years ago, when North and South America drifted away from Europe, the Rocky Mountains began to take shape. Erosion formed plains; river valleys appeared and became deeper; the valleys and passes of today were formed.

This region was later shaped by glaciation. About a million years ago, some glaciers existed in steep hollows at the upper end of several mountain valleys in the Crowsnest Pass. These were joined by glaciers from the Rock Range to the west. Roughly 500,000 years ago, a great valley glacier was formed, which soon included ice from Waterton Lakes and Glacier National Parks. From the Pass, a stupendous ice field over 300 metres deep reached as far as Lethbridge.

Later, a sheet of ice from Hudson Bay overtook the field and, in time, grew to cover half of North America. At the foot of the Rockies, the ice had a depth of some 150 metres. By some 20,000 years ago, this immense sheet of ice had receded to Lethbridge. (The last great Glacial Period, or, in common parlance, "Ice Age" began 72,000 years ago and ended 10,000 years ago). Also within this time period, a significant glacier (again with a depth of some 150 metres) proceeded down the Crowsnest Pass, depositing gravel terraces and benches from Crowsnest Lake to the Blairmore Gap.

Though perhaps drier, the climate after the last Ice Age was much like it is now. In caves above Crowsnest Lake—very close to the Alberta–British Columbia border— 22,000-year-old bones of horses, bison, lemmings, hoary marmots, and passenger pigeons have been discovered. At that time, an alpine grassland environment similar to today's already existed.

First Natives

Although human beings may have inhabited the Crowsnest Pass before and during the last Ice Age, proof of this will likely never be found. Ice and erosion would have destroyed any possible sites.

The last ice advance in the Pass occurred about 11,000 years ago. If humans were about then, as it appears, they would have had a lot of game to hunt in the alpine grassland: bison, caribou, horse, and mammoth, for instance.

Significant aspects of the prehistory of the area were uncovered in the course of various excavations during the 1970s, notably those undertaken by Dr. B.O.K. Reeves and his company, Lifeways of Canada. In 1973 alone, his workers identified over 250 prehistoric sites in the Pass, more than those ever found in an Alberta mountain valley. Gradually, valuable secrets have been revealed of an intricate record of cultures and land use over 11 millennia.

The first inhabitants to definitely occupy the Pass left records dating to roughly 9000 bc. Some broken tools found on a ridge near Frank reveal the presence at this time of members of the distinctive Clovis culture. Elsewhere in North America, during the latter centuries of the Ice Age, the Clovis people used sophisticated stone tools to hunt, kill, and process big game.

Next, there appeared in the Pass a number of hunting cultures, each with a distinctive technology. The first, the Old Cordilleran, appeared about 8000 BC. (This culture appeared in other mountainous districts of the continent as early as 13,000 bc.) Members of this culture in the Crowsnest used spear points of obsidian and basalt, volcanic rocks that probably came from Yellowstone National Park and near the Columbia River in the United States. Archeologists have concluded that travel and trade were organized extensively in these early times, and that they continued into the recorded, historic period.

From evidence gathered at over a dozen sites, it is known that the Agate Basin culture was represented in the Crowsnest around 7000 bc. Originally from the plains, Agate Basin people displaced the Old Cordilleran peoples. They used various kinds of traps on bison and other hoofed mammals. They became a distinctive mountain culture, hunting in the winter and probably fishing at Crowsnest Lake in the summer. They frequently travelled through the mountain passes. Their culture persisted until about 6000 bc, when it was relocated to the plains.

From 4000 to 3000 BC, people of the Mummy Cave culture occupied the plains and mountains. (Afterwards, they were to be found solely in the mountain valleys.) The Mummy Cave people used a special spear thrower, called the *atlatl*, which acted like a sling. The *atlatl* was a big improvement over throwing spears. Many sites in the Crowsnest have revealed Mummy Cave artifacts, especially those relating to the hunting of bison.

Small herds of bison, numbering up to 30 or so, were driven into corrals, backwaters, and bogs, where they were killed. A variety of hoofed mammals were hunted, and trapping occurred as well. Lodges made of grass mats were built. At Crowsnest Lake and elsewhere, Mummy Cave people established summer camps, where fishing took place.

Around 2500 bc, people from a culture known as McKean reached southern Alberta's plains from the Great Basin in the western United States. McKean peoples displaced the original peoples, who moved to the parkland fringes of Alberta and Saskatchewan. The new arrivals did not, however, displace the Mummy Cave people in the mountain valleys, a culture that lasted until around 1000 bc. The McKean peoples adapted very well, though gradually, to the plains; their culture became known as Pelican Lake.

The bow and arrow first appeared in North America in about 200 A.D. This Kootenay Native, shown here with his wife and niece in 1913, displays a more sophisticated version of the hunting tool invented by the Avonlea people.

About 1000 BC, Pelican Lake people finally reached the Crowsnest. Their sites were very common, indicating large populations at this time. During the Pelican Lake settlement period, the pattern of earlier times was followed. At Crowsnest Lake, large summer camps were maintained for the hunting of sheep, deer, bison, and elk; for fishing whitefish and suckers (with stone weirs, nets, and fish traps); and for trapping beaver, rabbits, and other fur-bearing animals. For equally practical reasons, spring and fall camps were established regularly on sites adjacent to the winter rangelands in the Bellevue/Burmis district. Winter settlement patterns were specific, and the emphasis was on bison hunting.

The Pelican Lake people travelled a great deal over mountain passes. They frequently visited Montana to obtain obsidian from the Yellowstone region and materials from stone quarries near Helena. Quarries near Fernie, BC, were frequented, too. Pelican Lake people would also hunt with their plains cousins at bison jumps, such as that at the famous Head-Smashed-In Buffalo Jump, a world heritage site.

In the late Pelican Lake period, a new culture called Besant advanced across the plains from the Minnesota-Iowa region. About 2,000 years ago, Besant peoples moved into the Saskatchewan and Missouri basins, displacing Pelican Lake peoples. They did not, however, settle in the occupied mountain areas.

It is possible that the Besant peoples were the ancestors of the Blackfoot of the plains. Coming from very advanced agricultural cultures in Illinois and Ohio, they brought with them new technology and an intricate social and economic system, including very long distance trade of stones from quarries in North Dakota and obsidian from Yellowstone National Park.

Prehistoric Kootenay Peoples and Their Ancestors

The Native people living in the Crowsnest region today are the Kootenay (or Kootenai). Unfortunately, there are few sites in the Crowsnest—or elsewhere in mountainous terrain—that relate directly to the prehistoric Natives called the Kootenay and their ancestors. Information about the Plains Natives is more abundant, though, and it helps shed some light on the Natives in the Crowsnest.

About ad 200, there was a major technological advance: the bow and arrow appeared in conjunction with a culture known as Avonlea. The Avonlea peoples were sophisticated bison hunters and excellent makers of stone tools. Up until that time, nothing as impressive as their stone-tipped projectiles had been produced by any other group. Avonlea inhabited both the plains and mountains.

Kootenay settlement during the last 1000 years featured much travel between the Kootenay Valley in British Columbia and the eastern slopes of the Rockies. Although significant summer camps were continued at Crowsnest Lake, major wintertime camps were established in the Kootenay Valley, outside the Crowsnest Pass.

The Kootenay told various early explorers that they had been forced out of the foothills, where they had been accustomed to winter, by the Blackfoot. Evidence shows that the Blackfoot did appear in the foothills around ad 1000. Moreover, the occurrence of a large number of traits of Plains Natives among the Upper Kootenay, such as decorative motifs, dress, and the use of the teepee, also supports the conclusion that the Kootenay originally inhabited eastern slopes of the foothills, as well as the Kootenay Valley.

Plains Blackfoot spent winters in the Rocky Mountain foothills near the Crowsnest Pass and elsewhere. Still, they did not regard mountainous lands as part of their territory. Tradition has it, however, that the Blackfoot made use of the Crowsnest Pass to stage raids into the BC Interior.

The subsistence cycle of the Kootenay after they obtained horses is of interest, particularly in the case of the Upper Kootenay, who frequently went eastwards onto the plains to hunt bison (which the Lower Kootenay groups seldom did).

From early spring to May, the Kootenay engaged in fishing. In May, women collected root vegetables and men hunted on a casual basis. In mid-June, a four-week expedition was undertaken to hunt bison in the foothills or on the plains. Hunting and berry-picking took up the rest of the summer. In September, on the eastern slopes of the Rockies, the bison were again hunted. Yet a third time, in January, the Kootenay hunted the great beasts, this time entirely by foot, using snowshoes.

Although the Upper Kootenay made use of many kinds of foodstuffs, they relied considerably on bison as their major food resource. Apart from meat, bison also provided hides for shelter and clothing, bones for tools and grease, and sinew for sewing. Since bison produce heavy coats of hair in winter, their hides were also used for winter clothing.

Chapter 2
A Route Through the Pass

*I*n 1792, the first fur-trading posts in Alberta were built by competing companies on the North Saskatchewan River. That winter, a few fur-traders lived with Native bands in their home areas. One of these was Peter Fidler, who headed off with a group of Peigans that lived in the foothills south of Calgary. He kept a detailed journal of his wintertime activities.

Near the Oldman River, Fidler encountered a group of Kootenay interested in trading. He followed them to The Gap, just 40 kilometres north of the Crowsnest Pass. They discussed with Fidler—the first white person they had seen—their regular eastward route through the mountains, strongly indicating the Crowsnest Pass.

In the 1840s, Father Pierre Jean de Smet worked as a missionary among the Kootenay in the Tobacco Plains area of northern Montana and southern British Columbia. In 1845, he travelled all the way to Rocky Mountain House to try to convince the Blackfoot to make peace with the Kootenay, who were very fearful after various clashes. During the trip, he passed very close to the Crowsnest Pass.

During later journeys, the intrepid priest entered the Pass when visiting the Elk River valley. He was the first white traveller in the Pass. In one letter, he wrote: "The fine river Des Chutes [the Elk River] comes roaring down and crosses the plain before it joins its waters to the McGillivray (Kootenay)…and having remarked large pieces of coal along the river, I am convinced that this fossil could be abundantly procured."[1]

By 1858, many individuals and groups advocated that the British government take over this property in British North America, then owned by the Hudson's Bay Company (HBC). The HBC's Charter, which granted it monopoly trading rights in, and ownership of, immense stretches of land in North America, was up for renewal. (Much of northern Quebec and northern Ontario and vast lands from Ontario to the Rocky Mountains were HBC-owned and were formally called Rupert's Land). Decision-making of a high order was on the British government's agenda.

A select committee was formed in England, and the Palliser expedition was sent to Canada as a fact-finding delegation. Its mandate was to obtain masses of factual information about western Canada. From 1857 to 1858, the expedition—sometimes made up of more than one group at a time—explored the prairies, mountains, parkland, and forests. The HBC's Charter was eventually renewed. The British government, however, did purchase all of Rupert's Land in 1870.

The first recognition of the Crowsnest Pass by that name resulted from the Palliser expedition's activities. Lieutenant Thomas Blakiston was ordered to determine if "Kootenay" Pass was in British territory. Following a personal dispute with Palliser, Blakiston left the main body. His later account called the pass he found the Crow Nest Pass. In fear of possible raids by Natives, he headed south between the Livingstone Range (which runs in a north-south axis about 5 kilometres east of Blairmore) and the Porcupine Hills (about 90 kilometres west-north-west of Lethbridge.) In so doing, he travelled through the mouth of the Crowsnest Pass.

In referring to the Pass, Blakiston wrote: "We know only that its eastern entrance is on the river of the same name, while it

An engraving of Jesuit missionary Father Pierre Jean de Smet, ca. 1873. Father de Smet was the first white traveller in the Crowsnest Pass and the discoverer of its coal.

emerges in the vicinity of the 'Steeples' or 'Mount Deception.'"[2] Later in the account, he added: "By report of the [Natives] it is a very bad road and seldom used."[3] Overall, Blakiston left the impression that no Natives lived in the Crowsnest Pass, but this was probably just a reflection of that particular time, when the bison population was low.

Indications are that Michael Phillipps was the first white person to cross through the Crowsnest Pass. An officer at Hudson's Bay Company posts in Idaho and Montana, he found himself unemployed when all HBC posts in the western United States were sold. In 1873, accompanied by a trapper, John Collins, he headed north up the Elk River valley to engage in some prospecting.

Lundbreck Falls, ca. 1920s. The eastern boundary of the Crowsnest Pass is generally considered to be near Lundbreck Falls, in Alberta.

For several days, the men camped at the eventual site of Fernie. They then headed north and found an old camping site, where Phillipps had camped in the 1860s. Here, Michel Creek empties into the Elk River. Phillips and Collins headed up Michel Creek for a few days. They came across some large trails, presumably made by Natives.

Phillipps wrote: "We found trees covered with buffalo hair and it was evident to both of us that we had passed through the Rocky Mountains without going over any range. This [was] the first trip ever made by what is now known as the Crow's Nest Pass."[4] Unfortunately, Phillipps left only a vague and incomplete account of this trip.

In 1873, too, W.S. Lees became established at the lake which bears his name (southeast of Hillcrest and Bellevue). He claimed that, that year, he went travelling from his ranch and discovered hot springs close to the eventual town of Frank, Alberta.

In the summer of 1874, Phillipps returned to the Pass with a miner named Morrissey and two other men. They arrived at and named Morrissey Creek south of Fernie and left with some coal. They named the next large stream they came across Coal Creek. Phillipps later wrote: "We could find nothing but coal and coal everywhere."[5] Then they came upon a creek with green lizards all about, which they named Lizard Creek.

In 1876, Phillipps and Morrissey again went prospecting in the Pass. Tired of seeing so much coal everywhere, they were delighted to go north of the Pass up the Bull River,

Canadian International Boundary Commission staff, ca. 1872 George M. Dawson, the well-known geologist who investigated the Crowsnest Pass in 1883, stands third from the right in the back row.

where they found some iron and gold deposits. Around the same time, the BC government gave a small grant to Phillipps to blaze a trail through the Pass. The trail was not properly maintained; it has sunk into oblivion.

Soon the Pass was truly opened, however, and it became a major connection between the mountains in the Kootenay region and the plains. It became an extensively used summer trail, "with horses and cattle from as far as Kamloops being driven through it. It became a matter of intense interest to the ranchers of the Pincher Creek and [Fort] Macleod district and is mentioned quite frequently in the early newspapers."[6]

In 1882, geologist George M. Dawson first visited the area. Although he only explored up to the eastern entrance of the Pass, he did locate one coal seam nearly a metre thick and another seam a little over a metre thick, a few kilometres below Lundbreck Falls.

The next year, Dawson entered the Crowsnest Pass and carried out a detailed geological examination. By this time, the Pass was popular for transportation, a very good trail with some bridges.

Building the Railway

As early as 1881, the Canadian Pacific Railway (CPR) had conducted an exploratory survey of the Crowsnest Pass. For military considerations, however, the federal government opposed building a main line so near the international boundary.

Two major groups actively promoted the building of a railway through the Crowsnest Pass. The first group of supporters were British Columbians in general (and Victoria residents in particular), who were witnessing a flow of wealth southward into the United States from mining operations in the Kootenays. Such development and the consequent funnelling away of funds appeared likely to expand with the building westward of the American Great Northern Railroad, which was planning feeder lines into Canada. Isolation from the Interior was also something of a factor for coastal residents who felt no connection with their hinterland.

The second major impetus to build the railway line came from the ranching community around Pincher Creek and Fort Macleod in southwestern Alberta. Although establishing a market for their cattle was one side of the coin, the other was the fear of being left at a dead end, particularly after the CPR line was built through Calgary, terminating at Coalbanks (Lethbridge).

From 1891 to 1895, railway charters were granted to build a railway through the Crowsnest Pass, but these were not acted upon. Finally, early in 1896, a subsidiary of the CPR announced that it was financially able to proceed with the line. It received a charter, subsidies, and land grants. Fort Macleod became the construction centre of the enterprise.

The official sod turning for the railway was held at Lethbridge on July 14, 1897. It was originally intended that the line reach as far as Nelson, BC. Construction began immediately, and along several fronts: from Lethbridge west, largely along the Oldman River; from Fort Macleod east and west; from Elko and Wardner, BC, east and west; and from Kootenay Lake east.

After two seasons of work, by fall 1898, the rails were in operation. They ran from Lethbridge to Kootenay Landing at the south end of Kootenay Lake, a distance of nearly 480 kilometres, of which 320 kilometres were in mountainous terrain.

During construction, the North-West Mounted Police (NWMP) assumed responsibility for policing the line; they were also sworn in as special BC police officers to enhance their authority. Considering that, at one point, 4000 men were engaged in work, there was remarkably little lawlessness.

The labourers were hard workers who enjoyed drinking ($10,000 worth of liquor was brought in every month). The Macleod Gazette once wrote: "They haven't the appearance of men over-burdened with this world's wealth, but they all possess good honest faces, and are decidedly superior to the ordinary navvies met with in the west."[7]

The size of the labour force varied from 1500 to 4000 men during construction. A considerable number of navvies were Chinese workers who also had experience building the western mountainous section of the main CPR line. Reportedly, a cholera epidemic among these workmen resulted in many deaths. The actual occurrence of such an epidemic is, however, unsubstantiated.

Following the death of two workers, an investigation was held into the construction of the railway. Conditions in the camps were found to be lamentable. At all camps, bunkhouses were overcrowded and unsanitary. Anywhere from 50 to 60 men occupied bunkhouses that measured only 7.3 metres by 12.2 metres each, with 2.1 metre ceilings and no ventilation. Wages were $1.75 a day, and board stood at 70 or 75¢.

Building the railway cost $19 million, though this was partially offset by a federal government subsidy of $3.4 million. The CPR also received a grant of coal lands, amounting to 15.5 square kilometres. The block of land chosen near Hosmer, BC, was later developed by the CPR.

In 1903, the Crow's Nest Railway was interrupted by the Frank Slide. But soon "a rail line had been pushed over the top of the slide and service was resumed. ...[It] was a steeply graded line over the rocks. ...[The] grade was so steep that helper engines had to be used westward over the Slide until the diesels came and altered the picture."[8]

The way out for Pass residents was the Spokane International Railway, which had a branch running from Yahk, BC, to Kingsgate at the US border. For several years, the main express train through Lethbridge and the Pass became the Spokane Flyer. By 1914, however, the Kettle Valley Railway was completed. Railcars could be ferried across Kootenay Lake to the railway on the far side. With this access to Vancouver, the Spokane Flyer disappeared.

Chapter 3
Towns Are Established

Although the initial discovery of coal in the Crowsnest Pass dated to the late 1840s, the valuable resource was not mined commercially until much later. With no railway handy, it was not economical to exploit the great "black diamond" deposits of the Pass. The arrival of the Crow's Nest Railway in the late 1890s, however, signalled the beginning of a new era for southwestern Alberta and southeastern British Columbia.

BC Mining Towns

Among the earliest discoveries of the valuable mineral was that at Coal Creek on the BC side of the Pass. Some mining took place there while the railway was being built. Also, some 10 kilometres to the west, log huts—soon dubbed the Old Town—were built in 1897. Thus it was that Fernie, the first settlement in the Crowsnest and in the East Kootenay mountains, came into being.

According to an old Native story, Fernie lay under a curse from the outset. The tale states that two brothers named Fernie, who were prospecting the area, took Native women as their partners. One brother, however, returned his companion to her band. The furious mother of the young woman placed a curse on the two men and on all their endeavours. For decades, dire happenings at Fernie seemed to support the truth of such a tale. (See chapter 6)

Situated on a broad flat beside the Elk River, Fernie has no local coal mines, and, except for a time when coke was manufactured there, Fernie has never had the appearance of a mining camp, unlike virtually all the other communities in the Pass. The Crow's Nest Pass Coal Company, which owned almost all the coal measures on the BC side of the Pass and those on significant adjacent lands in the Elk Valley and beyond, chose to make Fernie its headquarters, thus helping considerably to ensure the town's existence.

By 1900, there were several hotels in Fernie, 125 buildings in the Old Town, and 29 miners' cottages. There was a board of trade, a school with over 100 students, and 4 or 5 churches. Wooden sidewalks were also in place. In 1901, a census indicated that the town had 1640 residents. Despite upcoming disasters and grave setbacks, Fernie was there to stay.

In August 1904, Fernie was incorporated as a city. The Crow's Nest Southern Railway, a subsidiary of the Great Northern Railroad, reached the fledgling city in December of that year.

Coal Creek, a mining camp 10 kilometres east of Fernie, 1899. Coal Creek was established in 1897, when the Crow's Nest Railway was being built through the Pass.

Forty kilometres northeast of Fernie, the twin towns of Michel and Natal were established. In 1898, mining began at Michel, where a town arose. All of this activity was undertaken by the Crow's Nest Pass Coal Company. Mining operations near Michel proved to be very lucrative for many years.

Early on, hopes were dashed that Michel would become a "feeder" for Fernie. The distance between the towns was simply too great. Very much a company town, Michel was the site of much activity at the turn of the century. The Crow's Nest Pass Coal Company built cottages, a hotel, and a store. In 1901, coke ovens were installed locally. By then, the town had 476 residents.

In the fall of 1907, a new town was started just over a kilometre west of Michel. From the outset, when lots were sold, New Michel was an "open" town rather than a company-owned town. Soon the town had a bank, a school, three churches, nine stores, and a (short-lived) newspaper. When the CPR constructed a new station there, the name Natal was used. Despite general disapproval, the name stuck.

Plans were made to connect mining operations at Michel with those at nearby Morrissey, and not-so-near Coal Creek; Fernie would be the other destination. The proposed railway was dubbed the Morrissey, Fernie and Michel Railway (m.f. & m.r.).

The town of Fernie was named after two brothers who were both early prospectors in the Pass. Local folklore has it that a Native woman put a curse on the Fernies when one of them returned his Native partner to her band. Here, William Fernie poses in 1899.

Though it never became what it was supposed to be, as of the early 1950s, the 6.4 kilometre m.f. & m.r. claimed to be the world's smallest completely equipped railway.

Alberta Boomtowns

The development of coal in Alberta followed a different course from that in British Columbia, and mining was open to all investors. The first community to appear on the Alberta side of the Crowsnest Pass was Blairmore. On November 15, 1898, the Crow's Nest Railway reached the Tenth Siding, a section house and station for freight cars. (It was also called The Springs, in recognition of the nearby sulphur hot springs.) That day, the location was renamed Blairmore.

It is uncertain how the name came about. Some claim that "Blairmore" was an amalgam, presumably honouring two contractors, Blair and More, or a name with the suffix "more." Others maintain that the name honoured the minister of mines, A.G. Blair.

Two resident railway employees, Henry E. Lyon, the agent, and Felix Montalbetti, the section foreman, left their jobs and built cabins at Blairmore in the spring of 1899. They were the first settlers there. Lyon opened a store the following year. The coal properties on both sides of the railway were also bought in 1900.

Victoria Avenue, Fernie, 1899.

Elk Lumber Company mill, Fernie, ca. 1906. The mill employed many Fernie residents over the years.

With the 1901 opening of a mine at Frank, only 3 kilometres away, Blairmore boomed and quickly took shape as a community. Being situated in a wide valley, the Crowsnest Trough, the site boasted splendid scenery on all sides—a fine inducement to settlement. On September 3, 1901, Blairmore officially became a village. By year's end, some 257 people resided there, and three hotels had been erected.

In 1902, Blairmore's promising progress suddenly ground to a halt. On January 13th, storekeeper Lyon filed a caveat, claiming squatter's rights on land being divided into lots and sold. His claim and related legal complications effectively precluded Blairmore's growth until 1908. However, years of litigation almost wrecked the village, since no one could obtain clear title to land.

While the troubled town languished, the rest of the Pass was the scene of continuing activity on all fronts. Rather than settle in Blairmore, for example, many businessmen and workers chose to locate in nearby Frank, where no uncertainties over land ownership existed.

Blairmore's fortunes turned around in 1908. First, a plant built by the Rocky Mountain Cement Company began production. Then, a goodly number of miners fleeing strikebound Cape Breton settled in the town. Finally, West Canadian Collieries began developing a mine to the south of the townsite and set up its headquarters in the town. The company opened the significant Greenhill Mine to the north in 1913. This large and eventually very successful mine became the basis for continued development at Blairmore.

As of January 1910, the thriving town had 3 hotels, a newspaper, 2 schools, a bank, and 14 stores. It was fast becoming an important centre for Pass shoppers. That year, 9 business buildings and 200 residences were erected. The community soon featured an opera house, a customs office, the regional office of the Alberta government telephone service, and a new railway station, where the Spokane Flyer stopped on a regular basis.

By June 1910, 1200 people were employed at the mine, 150 at the brickyard, 400 at the cement plant, and 150 as carpenters and labourers. With the arrival of 1911, Blairmore's population stood at 2000 people. Not surprisingly, during the boom times— when substantial growth seemed destined to continue unabated—the Blairmore Enterprise conferred upon the town the title The Eldorado of the Golden West.

The coal mine at Frank, a short distance west, not only gave the community of Blairmore a boost, it also supported the town of Frank. This town had its origins in the summer of 1900, when a Blairmore miner discovered coal on Turtle Mountain, near his home town. He soon sold his claim to an entrepreneur named W.S. Gebo, whose business associate was H.L. Frank, a wealthy capitalist from Butte, Montana. The two men established the Canadian American Company to develop the deposits.

The town of Michel in 1919. It was founded in 1898.

Natal was established in 1907, and was originally called New Michel. Here are both Michel and Natal in 1930.

The Rocky Mountain Cement Works in Blairmore was a major economic force in the Alberta town for a number of years.

The town of Blairmore in 1950.

Mining operations at Turtle Mountain began in the spring of 1901. A railway spur to the mine was completed soon thereafter. The enterprising H.L. Frank had some two dozen cottages and a boardinghouse erected to accommodate miners and their families, and the town of Frank was started. The mines opened at Frank were the first to produce and ship coal on the Alberta side of the Crowsnest Pass.

The town's prospects appeared excellent indeed, and on September 10, 1901, Frank staged a lavish official opening of the town named after him. Some 1400 spectators and various dignitaries attended the celebrations and free banquet. Special trains arrived from various centres, including Cranbrook. Those present included the minister of the interior, Sir Clifford Sifton, and the Hon. F.G. Haultain, premier of the North-West Territories (Alberta and Saskatchewan). Frank had a population of 300 at the time of its opening, and over 500 lived there by spring 1903. That year, a deadly landslide—later called the Frank Slide—destroyed the buildings on the eastern flats, outside the town proper.

Contrary to common belief, the landslide did not spell the end of Frank. Mining resumed within a month, and a new tipple and washhouse were built by 1905. A new shaft mine was opened—though not on Turtle Mountain, where a huge wedge of rock had broken off, causing the Frank Slide. A zinc smelter was also constructed although it was never used. Additionally, the Canadian American Company bought the existing facilities at the hot springs nearby, and had built a hotel on the site. It was reputed to be one of the finest hotels in Canada. An elaborate stagecoach transported guests from the nearby railway to the hotel. For years, a prominent businessman from Blairmore drove the coach.

The local mine was shut down in 1911, when federal geologists warned that mining just might cause another slide. The original town soon disappeared and, nearby, the modern village of Frank began to take shape.

In following years, a host of mines appeared and disappeared throughout the eastern reaches of the Crowsnest Pass. Although American companies dominated mining, companies capitalized from Europe (especially France and Belgium) also operated. During the few years of this early boom, settlers often had houses built or they lived in company accommodation close to the mines. Accordingly, a total of 10 towns were established within a stretch of 22 kilometres on the Alberta side of the Pass. Some of these did not remain after the 1914 depression, but by 1906, in addition to Blairmore and Frank, the surviving towns of Bellevue, Coleman, and Hillcrest were all in existence.

Bellevue got off to a slow start compared to Blairmore and Frank, some 5 kilometres west. The moving force behind the founding of the town was J.J. Fleutot, an entrepreneur who organized West Canadian Collieries Ltd., an English company bankrolled by French interests. Soon after the turn of the century, Fleutot bought the Bellevue prospect, which, conveniently, was adjacent to the railway. One day, while gazing at the site of the

Front street, Bellevue, pre-1917.

prospective mine and town, Fleutot exclaimed, "Quelle belle vue!" ("What a beautiful sight!") Hence the town's name.

Fleutot himself retained ownership of a hotel built at the young community; 15 cottages were also erected, a clear indication that West Canadian intended its presence there to be a long-term one. Then, in 1907, Spokane backers founded the Maple Leaf Coal Company to develop a seam near the town. Following a survey, the former company offered town lots for sale. The Maple Leaf mine began operating in the fall of 1909. A feverish building spree took hold of the settlement, and, with the appearance of a large new West Canadian tipple, Bellevue's continued existence was apparently secure.

West to the Rocky Mountains from Blairmore, there is only one significant coal seam. There, 6 kilometres away, the town of Coleman made its appearance at the turn of the century. Isolated from the other communities of the Pass, Coleman retained much autonomy in various respects.

Residential street, Coleman, 1930.

Townsite lots were made available in 1903, but most residents continued to make tents their home; others occupied hotel rooms in Blairmore. That year, the International Coal and Coke Company began operations at the Dennison Collieries. In 1904, the town mushroomed, as many settlers decided there was a future for them in Coleman, after all. The community soon had the largest population in the area. Having received its name from Florence Coleman Flummerfelt, daughter of the townsite developer, Coleman was incorporated as a town in 1910.

Because of a business arrangement with a smelter at Greenwood, BC, International Coal installed over 200 beehive coke ovens at Coleman. The ovens were located within the townsite, alongside tracks parallel to the main street.

A newspaper journalist once noted that, during the years before diesel fuel use, the ovens' intense fires turned the coal of the Crowsnest into coke for use by the CPR's steam locomotives. He added: "Travellers arriving around midnight would get the shock of their lives on looking out and seeing the coke oven fires burning so fiercely. Some said that it

Residential street, Hillcrest, ca. 1920. The town was founded in 1905.

really was like being in hell itself."[1]

In 1900, Charles Plummer Hill, a US customs officer and an industrious, part-time American prospector of the area, discovered coal deposits at what became the Hillcrest mine site. By 1907, the fledgling community had its own railway station, post office, and school. Within a few years, almost 800 residents called Hillcrest home. As managing director of the Hillcrest Coal and Coke Company, Hill opened the mine in 1905. The mine was sold to Hillcrest Collieries in 1909. Five years later, a horrific mine disaster took place at the site.

Chapter 4
The Eastern Approach

he area adjacent to the Crowsnest Pass in Alberta is particularly notable for two sites: Head-Smashed-In Buffalo Jump and Fort Macleod, the first post of the North-West Mounted Police.

Head-Smashed-In Buffalo Jump

About 18 kilometres northwest of Fort Macleod (and about 160 kilometres south of Calgary) is one of the most remarkable and interesting sites on the prairies: Head-Smashed-In Buffalo Jump. Worldwide attention has been accorded the site in the Porcupine Hills since it was designated a national historic site in 1968 and a UNESCO world heritage site in 1981. To considerable acclaim, the $10 million interpretive centre was officially opened by Prince Andrew and the former Duchess of York in July 1987.

The buffalo jump and interpretive centre are symbolic of both the inventiveness of the Plains Natives and their heavy dependence on the bison for all necessities. At one time, 60 million bison roamed the plains. During hunts, the ancestors of today's Natives would drive the great shaggy creatures into marshes, snowdrifts, or enclosures. The technique of stampeding bison over cliffs was also used, as it was in prehistoric Europe. These cliffs, or buffalo jumps, are found throughout North America and are especially common along the eastern edge of the foothills in Colorado, Montana, and Alberta.

What makes Head-Smashed-In such a remarkable buffalo jump is its extent, its fine state of preservation, and the length of time it was in use. The most complex buffalo jump in existence, it "is one of the most cunning traps and one of the most brilliant ruses devised by prehistoric man in pursuit of big game."[1]

During initial excavations in 1965, led by Dr. B.O.K. Reeves, digging proceeded nine metres deep; at that point, bedrock was reached. Slaughtered bison bones dating to the fourth millennium bc were disinterred. Regular use of the buffalo jump dates to about 3750 bc. Although today the grey sandstone cliff stretches directly upward for 11 metres, at the time it was first used, it was twice this height; a mound of bison bones, artifacts, and dirt gradually built up over the centuries of use.

In Blackfoot, the site is known as Estipah-sikikini-kots, or "where he got his head smashed in." According to legend, a young man wanted the best possible view of the great beasts falling to their deaths, so he positioned himself under a ledge partway up the cliff. The herd that stampeded that day was so large, however, that the animals piled up very high and buried the young man. When he was discovered, his skull was smashed in.

Dr. B.O.K. Reeves began initial excavations of Head-Smashed-In Buffalo Jump in 1965.

Cliff face of Head-Smashed-In Buffalo Jump, 1964. Today, the cliff is 11 metres high. It was originally twice this height.

Among experts, there is still much sense of wonder at the gathering and controlling of the bison herds. A senior archeologist with the Archaeological Survey of Alberta, Jack Brind, once stated: "The more I study, the more I get boggled at how they pulled these things off. ...It really is a testimony to an enormous amount of ingenuity, sophistication and knowledge."[2]

The hunts usually occurred during the fall or early winter, and as many as 500 people would take part in the endeavour. The bison would sometimes be directed toward the jumps over a period of several days. Great care would be taken by the Natives to remain downwind to keep their scent from the bison; as an added precaution, hunters would smear grease and sage over their bodies to disguise their scent.

Leading to the cliff are "drive lanes." These lanes consisted of rock cairns designed to steer the bison in the desired direction. At most jumps, there were only two drive lanes to funnel the bison toward a cliff. At the so-called gathering basin of Head-Smashed-In, however, a maze of over 30 intersecting drive lanes was used, these using more than 12,000 cairns. Not all lanes lead to Head-Smashed-In; some lead to other cliffs and some to faraway buttes. The complexity of the system is unique.

The drive lanes were in a giant V formation, the open end being the herd in the gathering basin, the vertex being at the cliff face. V formations were up to four or five kilometres in length at Head-Smashed-In.

Eyewitness accounts say that brush was stuck into the cairns to help keep bison in the correct drive lanes. Strips of rawhide, designed to blow in the wind, may have been attached to the brush. To begin the drive, careful runners camouflaged in antelope clothing or in bison hide and headdress would try to get the herd moving in the desired direction. To keep the bison together, hunters would often don coyote hides and threaten the calves. Other people would line the drive lane and wave bison robes to keep directing the herd toward the cliff.

The overall role of the runners was crucial, demanding, and dangerous, with runners continuing their work until the last possible moment. Observers found the skills of the runners phenomenal. Of the Assiniboine's runners, fur-trader Alexander Henry wrote: "Their gestures so closely resembled those of the animals themselves that had I not been in on the secret, I should have been as much deceived as the buffalo."[3]

As the herd approached the cliff, the stampede became more and more frenzied, with the animals bunched in closer and closer together. Only the lead animals could see clearly, and what they saw as they approached the cliff was an optical illusion, for they saw a continuous prairie carpet stretching to the horizon. On and on they thundered, past people waving bison robes and shouting. Then, the 450 kilogram animals hurtled over the cliff. As many as 500 bison per drive might fall to their deaths.

At the cliff bottom, animals still alive were finished off by spears or arrows. Then the kill would be dragged down to the nearby flats. Bison flesh would be roasted on hearths or dried in the sun. Bones would be pulverized and boiled to render grease. Undoubtedly, most of the dried meat was mixed with berries and grease to form pemmican, which would be stored in large bags for use in coming months and even years, if necessary.

Probably the Peigan, expert hunters, conducted the last drive at Head-Smashed-In Buffalo Jump about 1860, when the site was abandoned. Not long after, prairie bison were nearly exterminated by whites.

Fort Macleod

Recruitment of a mounted police force for the Canadian plains began in September 1873. The major factor prompting formation of the North-West Mounted Police was public outrage about the Cypress Hills Massacre in May 1873, when over 30 Natives were slaughtered by trappers. Fear of possible retaliation against whites resulted in the force being hastily organized and dispatched to Lower Fort Garry, 32 kilometres north of Red River (Winnipeg).

In January 1874, Prime Minister Alexander Mackenzie authorized Commissioner George A. French to conduct an expedition with two objectives: to arrest the murderers and to eradicate the pernicious liquor trade. To facilitate the expedition, French recruited and trained 150 more men in eastern Canada. The two NWMP contingents rendezvoused in June at Fort Dufferin, Manitoba, the point of departure.

On July 8, 1874, the mounted police set out on what later became known as the March West. Six divisions, "A" through "F", accounted for the 274 men and officers present. The first destination was scheduled to be Fort Whoop-Up, a notorious whisky-trading post, 1300 kilometres distant.

On September 9, the NWMP reached the confluence of the Oldman and Belly Rivers, but no fort was there. Commissioner French then headed south to Fort Benton, Montana, where he learned that Fort Whoop-Up was at the juncture of the St. Mary and Oldman Rivers. There, too, he recruited Jerry Potts, the great scout of Blood and Scots parentage.

Returning to the Sweet Grass Hills, where his tired force was recuperating, French commanded two divisions to ride with him to Fort Pelly (near the present Saskatchewan-Manitoba boundary). The three remaining divisions were ordered to proceed to Fort Whoop-Up under the command of James F. Macleod, the assistant commissioner. (Earlier, in Saskatchewan, one division had diverged to make their way northwest to Fort Edmonton.)

When the mounted police reached the fort, they discovered that the whisky-traders had long since fled, having heard of the might facing them. The Cypress Hills murderers were nowhere to be found, either; they had fled across the border.

On October 13, the great March West ended when, on the advice of Jerry Potts, Macleod's 150 men reached a sheltered lowland along the Oldman River, some 32 kilometres upriver from Fort Whoop-Up. This, said Potts, was just the place to build a fort, and the men got to work building what became known as Fort Macleod.

The outside walls of the fort were erected by placing 3.6 metre logs, plastered with mud, upright in trenches nearly a metre deep. Winter was fast coming, so sod served as roofs, and dirt as floors. A square, 60 metres across, was encompassed by living quarters, stores, a kitchen, a hospital, stables, and a blacksmith shop.

Lieutenant-Colonel James F. Macleod, Commissioner of the North-West Mounted Police, 1876-80. Macleod led a mounted police force to Fort Whoop-Up in 1874 and then proceeded to build the first NWMP post at Fort Macleod. The welfare of his men was always one of his priorities.

The hospital and stables were built first. As Colonel Macleod wrote in his report: "I had made up my mind…that not a single log of men's quarters should be laid till the horses, as well as the sick men, were provided for. The men's quarters will then be proceeded with, and then those of the officers."[4] The fort was completed before Christmas.

Conditions were far from enviable. One policeman wrote to his father in October 1876: "This is the worst Fort I have been to yet, for comfort. The buildings are miserable, mud floors and mud roofs, so that when it rains there is a devil of a mess."[5] Plank floors did not appear until later in the year, when a sawmill was established.

Fort Macleod, built in 1874, was the first NWMP post on the plains. It is depicted here in 1875 drawing by R.B. Nevitt for the Canadian Illustrated News.

Early on, regular patrols were instituted. In fact, only two weeks after the arrival of the NWMP, some whisky traders were arrested 65 kilometres to the north at Pine Coulee. Patrols also went as far south as the Canada–United States border. Such patrols were always on the move, because the Natives travelled the plains in search of bison, and the whisky traders kept on the tracks of the Natives.

The vigilance and determination of the mounted police were evident from the first, and benefits were soon noticed. The trade in whisky virtually ceased, as did drunkenness, and nearly all the whisky traders not already in Montana withdrew across the border. Indeed, the "effect was almost magical, and the Rev. John McDougall, when he visited Fort Macleod on New Year's Eve, spoke of the change which had come over the country as 'a miracle wrought before our eyes.'"[6]

Very good relations were established with the Natives. A friendly, respectful relationship came into being between Macleod and Crowfoot, the famous chief of the Blackfoot Confederacy. An officer, Sir Cecil Denny, later wrote: "The Indians…got over their fear of us, many councils being held. They were told the reason for our coming, and were glad to have whisky abolished. Large camps of many hundred Blackfoot, Bloods and Peigans near us are on very friendly terms."[7]

In 1884, because the Oldman River changed course, the fort and town were forced to move. The site chosen was about four kilometres to the west, on bench land over-

North-West Mounted Police scouts, Fort Macleod, 1890.

looking the river and on the south side of it. The new buildings encompassing the parade grounds stretched 147 metres by 77 metres. Lumber was used throughout, resulting in greater comfort.

At the time the first fort was being built, a small village began to take shape beside it. The main structure was the I.G. Baker store, a favourite rendezvous for the police, many of whom had accounts there, despite the high interest charged. A billiard room/confectionery soon opened. By the end of the first winter, some shacks and several other businesses were in evidence, including a general store, a carpenter's shop, a shoemaker's shop, a blacksmith's shop, and—surprisingly, perhaps, though within the law of the day—one or two gambling establishments.

For a few years, Fort Macleod was the most important settlement in southern Alberta. Situated along the Fort Benton–Edmonton trail, it was not only the headquarters of the NWMP for a while, it was the chief centre of a thriving trade in bison skins until the late 1870s. Construction of the CPR through Calgary, however, ended Fort Macleod's standing as the major distribution centre in the region. Things improved somewhat when the Calgary–Fort Macleod line was built; things were even better when the town became part of the Crow's Nest Railway and an important railway junction. From the outset, Fort Macleod was very important to the local ranching community.

North-West Mounted Police artillery detachments, "D" and "H" divisions. Fort Macleod, 1890.

Fort Macleod buildings and residences, ca. 1875. A town quickly appeared at the site of the original fort after its founding in 1874.

Main street, Fort Macleod, 1898. The fort and town were relocated to their present site in 1884.

The settlement was incorporated as a town in December 1892. Although "Fort" was dropped from the name at the time, it was tacked on again some years later, and it remains yet. By 1892, many businesses were already operating, spanning the spectrum from bowling and target shooting to a hot bath/hairdressing operation and a produce store. By 1906, the population amounted to about 1000; by 1911, the figure stood at 2510. At this time, business lots along the main street cost $250 to $350 per front foot.

Chapter 5
The Western Approach

B C's East Kootenay region, which lies west of the Crowsnest Pass, has seen a rich past—from a gold rush, to unsolved murders, to a notable NWMP post.

Fisherville and Wild Horse Creek

Some 16 kilometres north of Fort Steele are the remains of a townsite known as Fisherville; it lies along Wild Horse Creek. This area of the East Kootenay was explored over the years by adventurous individuals, including David Thompson, Joseph Howse, Sir George Simpson, James Sinclair, Father Pierre Jean de Smet, and Captain John Palliser.

In late 1863, during the Cariboo gold rush, a prospector named Linklater discovered gold at the foot of Fisher Mountain. Over 20 men made their way into the Wild Horse area in early spring 1864. They had heard of the strike and wanted to check things out. By June, over 500 miners were located in the flats; virtually all were Americans.

By the fall, over 1000 miners and prospectors were in the vicinity. A boomtown, Fisherville, soon took shape. It boasted four restaurants, which charged $14 to $18 a week; there were also many cafes and boardinghouses. Roughly 50 buildings, including saloons and gambling houses, were in evidence. A large brewery appeared, and it operated round the clock.

About this time, a man called Shirt Collar Bill had a placer claim marked on its upstream boundary by a huge drift log, some 45 metres long. The creek he was mining rose one night, and the log drifted to the upstream boundary of the finest piece of ground around, belonging to one Scotty or Shorty. Shirt Collar claimed the ground and began to work it, maintaining that Divine Providence had awarded it to him. Scotty/Shorty, however, soon came along. He placed a great deal of powder under the log and blew it up. He then suggested that Shirt Collar search for his precious boundary marker in a very hot spot.

Although strikes were also made at several nearby creeks, most activity was centred at Wild Horse Creek. One of the earliest miners, Robert C. Dore, had a claim that produced $522,000 in three years. He was the first to install a hydraulic plant on Wild Horse.

At first, the Wild Horse gold rush was almost entirely an American affair. The only road leading out of the vicinity initially had an American destination, Colville, Washington. By 1865, though, the Colony of British Columbia dispatched Peter O'Reilly, a notable frontier judge, to administer justice. By the time O'Reilly arrived, a

At its height, the town of Wild Horse catered to a population of up to 5000 people. It is shown here in 1888.

rough set of laws had already been drawn up; these were enforced by a vigilante committee, but little violence took place.

Also in 1865, it was discovered that the gravel bench on which the town was situated was rich in gold. The buildings were torn down or burnt, and the townsite was turned into piles of rocks. The town was moved farther up the hill it rested on, and was renamed Wild Horse.

The gold rush proper was of short duration. During the height of the rush in 1865, some observers estimated that as many as 5000 men camped in the Wild Horse area. That same year, the shallow placer diggings were cleaned out to the extent of millions of dollars worth of gold. With shaft or hydraulic mining the next step, many miners abandoned Wild Horse for the reported wealth of other locations, such as the Columbia Big Bend. A few hundred men, mostly Chinese, stayed on, and some Canadians arrived.

By 1873, hardly anyone remained at the creek. Today, beyond a few foundations, only a cemetery marks the site of the one-time booming location. Estimates of placer gold taken during the rush vary from $6 million to $25 million.

Galbraith's Ferry

As men poured in from the United States, they had to cross the Kootenay River to

Chief Isadore maintained that his fellow band member, Kapula, was innocent of the murder of two miners. Kapula was eventually acquitted. The chief poses with Kootenay Natives at Fort Steele, in 1888.

get to the gold fields. Seeing a good business opportunity, John Galbraith started operating a ferry across the river in June 1864. The charge was $5 per crossing. The ferry remained a family business until 1888, when a bridge was built across the river.

Galbraith settled at a spot near the junction of Wild Horse Creek and the Kootenay River. In addition to the ferry, he and his brother, Robert, also ran a store and conducted pack trains. The little settlement came to be known as Galbraith's Ferry. One of the immigration officers who served there was Charles Mair, author of Tecumseh, and a well-known poet.

From the ferry, three trails led southward and westward. One arrived at Walla Walla, Washington, via Joseph's Prairie (Cranbrook). Another trail led to Tobacco Plains and Montana. The third trail was the famous Dewdney Trail, a pack route which stretched from Fort Hope on the Fraser River to Galbraith's Ferry.

In 1884, two placer miners, named Kemp and Hylton, were murdered and robbed of their pokes at Deadman's Creek, near Wild Horse. A provincial constable named Anderson conducted an intensive investigation. At long last, in early March 1887, he arrested a Kootenay man, Kapula (or Kapla), and jailed him at the small settlement at Galbraith's Ferry.

Edward S. Curtis, a renowned photographer of North American Natives, took this photo of a Kootenay woman in 1910.

On the eleventh day of the month, Kootenay Chief Isadore and 30 armed warriors headed to the jail. There, they confronted Anderson and the local justice of the peace. An angry Isadore maintained that Kapula was innocent and had been wrongfully arrested. Although Anderson and the justice of the peace insisted that Kapula must stand trial, the Natives forcibly took the keys and released the prisoner. Isadore then informed the men that they should leave the district, if they wanted to keep their scalps. The men did. White settlers barricaded their homesteads and, greatly frightened, asked for government assistance.

Serious discontent among the Kootenay band had been simmering for some time. The prevailing bitterness originally resulted from the fact that they had accepted a reserve, but it was too small for the purposes of grazing their cattle and horses. For some years, this was not an issue because the owner of Joseph's Prairie, a large piece of land, let the livestock graze there. But when this land was sold in 1885, the new owner, Colonel James Baker, wanted the land for his own ranch. He ordered Chief Isadore to remove his stock. Isadore utterly refused to do so, and the animals remained on the tract of land.

After an investigation, Inspector Superintendent William Herchmer reported that the young Kootenay men were very upset with the settlers and showed it; he reported, too,

Mary Madeline Isaacs was the grand-daughter of Eneas (Big Knife), chief of the Elmo Kootenay.

that the band could certainly field 350 well-armed warriors, if it so wished. Homesteaders seriously feared a rising by the Natives. The federal government decided that something had to be done, and it concluded that a detachment of mounted police should be sent to preserve peace in the district.

In late May 1887, Superintendent Samuel Benfield Steele received orders in Fort Macleod to hold himself in readiness to travel to British Columbia with 2 officers and 75 non-commissioned officers and constables.

Sam Steele was larger than life. Born in 1851 at Purbrook, Ontario, he learned how to ride, shoot, wrestle, and box. At age 14, he lied about his age and enlisted in the militia during the time of the Fenian raids from the United States. As a militia volunteer, he came west during the 1869–70 Red River Rebellion. He was the third man to sign on with the North-West Mounted Police, when it was established in 1873. Steele was involved with virtually every notable event of western Canadian history: primarily, the great March West, the North-West (or Riel) Rebellion, and the building of the CPR.

On June 26, the mounted police's "D" division under Steele left for Golden, BC, aboard a special train, arriving on June 28. The force left Golden on July 18 and travelled

North-West Mounted Police camp, Crowsnest Lake, 1887. From 1887 to 1888, the NWMP occupied a post at Galbraith's Ferry, near the Pass, to improve Native-White relations.

south along an old pack trail; at Upper Steamboat Landing on Lake Windermere on July 23 the mounted police met Robert Galbraith. Under his direction, the force reached Galbraith's Ferry on August 1.

Land on the plateau was leased from the Galbraiths. The site overlooked the junction of all significant trails in the area. Steele directed the building of a fort. Eight log buildings were erected, including barracks, officers' quarters, a guardroom, cells, sergeants' mess, quartermaster stores, a stable, and a smithy and saddlery shop. The fort was the first mounted police post west of the Rocky Mountains.

Beneficial effects arising from the force's arrival were soon most apparent. As Superintendent Steele wrote in his annual report: "As soon as possible I communicated with Indian Chief Isadore and with favorable results. The Indians soon began to visit the camp out of curiosity, and were more civil to the whites than formerly. The advent of the police caused confidence to take the place of alarm which had been felt during the winter and early spring by the whites."[1]

Generally good relations between the mounted police and Natives were significantly solidified with the results of the Kapula affair. Steele persuaded Chief Isadore to bring

Fort Steele, ca. 1888. The community of Galbraith's Ferry changed its name to Fort Steele to honour the popular Superintendent Sam Steele, who commanded a post at the community.

Traffic bridge, Fort Steele, 1895.

Kapula in for trial. Presiding himself, Steele released the man for lack of evidence. Convinced that Kapula was innocent, Steele attributed the murders to white renegades.

A year after their arrival, the mounties and police were recalled to Fort Macleod. The Natives were content, and the whites were no longer afraid. At Steele's suggestion, farm implements and feed grain had been provided to Chief Isadore's band. Steele had seen to it that irrigation ditches were constructed for the Natives at St. Eugene Mission, where he also had ensured the setting up of an industrial school for Native children. During his stay, Steele also established a mail service by dispatch riders, and provided mounted patrols along the vicinity's wagon road.

Sam Steele was a local legend in the Crowsnest Pass. He was the third man to join the North-West Mounted Police when it was founded in 1873, and played a part in almost every momentous historical event in western Canada.

Sam Steele made a great impression on the people of the area around Galbraith's Ferry. Unanimously, the district population decided to rename the location to honour him, and it became Fort Steele.

The mounted police division left Galbraith's Ferry on August 9, 1888. Steele led his men east through the Crowsnest Pass, following an old Native trail. He wanted to see how feasible the route was and kept careful notes. The division travelled the 312 kilometres to Fort Macleod in nine days. As a result of Steele's endeavours, regular police patrols began

Main street, Cranbrook, 1899. Cranbrook had its origins in 1897 when several establishments were built

to keep the Crowsnest trail open; it soon became the most popular route for travel into British Columbia.

Joseph's Prairie

The first name given to the location that is now Cranbrook was A'qkis qa'ktleet. This name applied to a Kootenay village there. It was an excellent spot in which to live, a flat and grassy plain, with good sources of water nearby. A small, steep hill, Isadore's Hill, served as a lookout from which enemy bands, particularly Peigans, could be spotted. With the arrival of avid gold-seekers, the plain was commonly called Joseph's Prairie, after the current Kootenay chief.

The great explorer David Thompson first explored the Kootenay and Columbia Rivers in British Columbia from 1807 to 1809. For over 50 years afterward, however, there was very limited exploitation of the wealth of the East Kootenays. And exploratory activity after Thompson amounted to little in terms of promoting economic activity.

The Wild Horse Creek gold rush stimulated businesses and settlement in the East

Cranbrook in 1906. The town was originally the site of a Kootenay settlement called "A'qkis qa'kleet." It was commonly referred to as Joseph's Prairie, after the Kootenay chief.

Cranbrook in 1912.

Kootenay region. In conjunction with the gold rush, the Oregon Boundary Agreement of 1846 necessitated construction of an all-Canadian route from the Pacific coast to the far-away Kootenays. By 1865, the Dewdney Trail from Hope to Galbraith's Ferry was finished. The trail opened up commerce and improved access between the coast and eastern British Columbia.

The Dewdney Trail crossed Joseph's Prairie (near which were some mining settlements). The grassy plain was in an excellent location, enjoying access to mountain passes to the north, south, and east.

In the late 1870s, cattle ranching was introduced to the region. In 1885, when Colonel James Baker bought the grazing lands at Joseph's Prairie, he renamed the property Cranbrook, after his hometown in England. At the location, a post office, a customs house, and a supply store opened. Cranbrook became something of a rendezvous for trappers and miners.

In spring 1897, Colonel Baker had his lands laid out and surveyed; a land office was established. The CPR railway survey proved to run through his property, which became the eventual basis for the city of Cranbrook. That year, a local sawmill was built to meet the needs of the CPR and of the growing town's settlers and businesses. A hotel was also opened.

In late July 1898, the first train of the CPR-owned Crow's Nest Railway reached Cranbrook. Local residents were overjoyed. At long last, the railway was a reality, and the town was about to become a prosperous and significant railway divisional point.

In 1898, the Cranbrook Herald appeared. A brewery opened the following year. The 1901 census set the population of Cranbrook at 1196. That year was a busy one for the vicinity; three hotels, a school, a hospital, a sawmill, a slaughterhouse, two general stores, a bakery, a livery stable, a meat market, and a bank were all built then.

In 1903, provincial government offices were relocated to Cranbrook from Fort Steele. In November 1905, Cranbrook was incorporated as a city. Heavy railway activity and an expanding and diversifying forest industry provided steady growth. As of 1910, some 23 sawmills operated in the region. The 1911 census demonstrated that over 3000 people called Cranbrook home.

Chapter 6
Accidents and Catastrophes

I t appears that almost every imaginable kind of disaster has afflicted Crowsnest Pass communities at one time or another. Calamity has battered the area in the form of mudslides, landslides, avalanches, fires, floods, rockfalls, and mine explosions.

Floods

Spring floods in the Pass have been the result of heavy snowfalls melting over relatively short periods of time. In 1897, floods caused much damage in this area. Two years later, the Elk River ruined the Canadian Pacific sawmill. Generally speaking, the eastern side has suffered more from flooding over the years.

When the Crowsnest River rises, its waters directly threaten harm to Coleman, Blairmore, Frank, and the Bellevue flats (locally called Bellevue Riverbottom). Flooding and consequent damage have hit these towns the hardest. Bellevue proper and Hillcrest, situated as they are on elevated land, have been quite safe from flooding.

The first major flood was in June 1923. Coleman was hit worst. West Coleman and Italian Town were transformed into lakes; the heart of the town was also flooded. The river washed away railway tracks; the East Coleman bridge collapsed; one house was whisked out into the river. Considerable damage occurred at Frank and Blairmore, and Bellevue's lower section was flooded. Highway bridges were washed away. A long section of railway track was washed out, effectively isolating the Pass for a few days. Surprisingly, no lives were lost, though there were a few casualties.

The next big flood occurred in early May 1942. Spring was late in coming that year, but there was enough rain to cause the river and creeks to overflow once again. Blairmore saw the most damage, though parts of Frank and Coleman were affected as well. In Blairmore, two creeks cascaded into town, "washing out their banks, undermining houses and taking out culverts and bridges. The low places were flooded and basements were filled by water rising through the subsoil."[1]

As a result, measures were undertaken to prevent flood damage in the future. The Crowsnest River was dredged by power machinery. Town councils were careful to clear out culverts every spring before high water levels occurred.

On the BC side of the Pass, torrential rains have occasionally caused serious mudslides. Heavy clay deposits on hillsides can flow downward during downpours and block railway lines and roads. Fernie has been cut off in such a manner several times. Although

A flood at Natal. Floods have been a recurring event in the Crowsnest Pass area. Flooding has been less severe on the BC side of the Pass.

A flood at Coleman in 1923, the first major one in the Pass.

Dominion Avenue, Frank, before the deadly Frank Slide of 1903.

avalanches pose little danger in this area, in late 1912, a mixed mass of snow and rock did slide down to Coal Creek, where it damaged property and killed six men.

The Frank Slide

At the advent of the twentieth century, the coal industry was a very important component of economic activity in Alberta. Although significant amounts of coal were mined in a number of areas, the Crowsnest Pass soon became the most productive mining region in the province. During the early years of the century, one of the top-producing mines in the Pass was at the town of Frank. Yet it was not coal production but the awesome forces of nature that would briefly focus worldwide attention on the little town in 1903.

Named after H.L. Frank, its founder, the town had a population of over 500 by the spring of 1903. The townsite was just south of Turtle Mountain, on a small flat that was angled between the Oldman River (or Crowsnest River) and Gold Creek. The river skirted the base of the mountain, where it joined with the creek.

Nearly all business establishments and most residences were located on the townsite proper. Across Gold Creek, on the eastern flats, were a dozen more residences and several business establishments.

Nothing unusual occurred at Frank on April 28, 1903. The miners working the day

Just after the Frank Slide. Workers just released from mines are being escorted to a hospital by rescue workers.

shift completed their labours without incident. The evening was similarly uneventful and ordinary.

At midnight, Joseph Chapman, a Welsh foreman, and 16 men assembled on Dominion Avenue and made their way to the mine entrance across the river. Their work centred on safe maintenance of the tunnels and equipment for the day crew. Not long after they disappeared into the depths of Turtle Mountain, a freight train from Macleod arrived to pick up some coal cars. The train was required to lay over on the spur for an hour or so in order to facilitate the progress of the Spokane Flyer, which was behind schedule on its Lethbridge-Spokane run.

At 4:10 am, there was a very brief, ominous rumbling from the mountain towering over Frank. Immediately, a dreadfully loud sound filled the valley—75 million tonnes of rock split off the mountainside and hurtled and smashed toward the town. About a minute and a half later, the mighty mass of limestone and shale had completed its destructive course.

The huge wedge of rock that broke loose from Turtle Mountain was some 150 metres thick, 650 metres high, and 900 metres wide. Much of it was in the form of boulders. The rock fortunately missed the town proper, but dealt death and destruction to the eastern flats. There, some 76 men, women, and children perished, including a dozen

These men are rebuilding the railway to the mine at Frank after the 1903 slide.

labourers who had recently arrived to complete a spur line from the nearby town of Lille to the CPR tracks.

The engineer of the freight train parked at the mine tipple reacted swiftly when he heard the first indications of a slide. His speeding train narrowly escaped destruction.

The men inside the mine were trapped when the mine portal was destroyed and buried. After hours of arduous digging—with the air supply almost exhausted—they managed to tunnel to the outside: all 17 survived.

The mine reopened some weeks later as miners and other townspeople began returning to Frank. There was no evidence that another slide was imminent. Nonetheless, the mine was closed forever in 1911, when federal geologists warned that mining operations might precipitate another deadly slide. The original town soon ceased to exist. Just outside the immediate vicinity of the slide, another small centre took shape, the modern village of Frank.

Fires

Until about 1940, forest fires posed a distinct threat to the whole Pass district. In 1902, half of the town of Michel burnt down from a fire caused by careless workers. In 1904, during a very dry spell, a forest fire began at the Great Northern Railroad right-

The disastrous 1908 fire at Fernie. Almost all of the city was destroyed. Six to 10 people may have perished during the inferno.

Fernie following the disastrous fire of 1908. Almost every building in town was destroyed by the blaze. Demonstrating great tenacity, Fernie residents immediately set about rebuilding their city. Wooden structures were no longer allowed.

Another view of the devastating fire of 1908 in Fernie.

of-way and devastated the whole Elk Valley; it raged into Alberta before it was stopped.

On April 29, 1904, a fire started in a general store in Fernie. It spread rapidly. Before long, virtually the whole business section—including 10 hotels—was in ruins. Six complete blocks were wiped out. The town then experienced a building boom.

Disaster struck Fernie again on August 1, 1908, with a vengeance. Powerful winds fanned a forest fire toward the city. The flames spread quickly once it reached the city of 6000 people. Within two hours, Fernie was no more. Apart from a small group of buildings separated from the town by an open expanse of lawns, all structures, except for two buildings, burnt to the ground. Reports of deaths set the figure variously from 6 to 10, but the actual number would never be definitely known.

The people of Fernie started to rebuild immediately. The "boom days were still with them, and the numerous smelters were crying for more and more coke. [People] rebuilt the eleven hotels, the brewery, the schools, the business blocks and the homes. All new buildings had to be of stone, brick, or concrete…the Fernie Brick Company [turned] out twenty thousand bricks a day, while two hundred and fifty carloads of cement were brought in."[2]

This photo shows the pumphouse and No. 2 mine entrance at the Hillcrest Mine on June 19, 1914, one day after an explosion in the mine took the lives of 189 men.

Then, in 1910, the whole area north of Blairmore and Coleman was ruined by a fire, while another blaze raged near Passburg and Burmis. In 1920 and 1921, fires swept across from north of Michel through Deadman Gap and around the foot of Crowsnest Mountain.

A great many fires broke out during the Great Depression of the 1930s; it is believed that many were set by people who desperately needed fire-fighting work. Since the late 1930s, most fires have been quickly brought under control, fire prevention and fire-fighting measures having been given very serious attention by governments.

Mining Disasters

Industrial fatalities have plagued the Pass for many years. Of the towns that continued to exist after the 1914 depression, only Blairmore has been spared from catastrophe.

The first disaster occurred at Coal Creek, near Fernie, on May 22, 1902. A terrific explosion ended the lives of 128 men, making the sad event one of the great mining disasters of the world. Many of the workers were married men who had not yet arranged

These coffins are ready for the burial of those killed in the 1914 Hillcrest Mine Disaster. At the time, it ranked as the third worst mine disaster in the world.

for homes suitable for their wives and children, who were living elsewhere at the time. It must be taken into account that the "possibility of an explosion had probably not been seriously considered up to that time and few precautions had been taken, for apparently many of the men smoked in the mine—one of the greatest offenses in modern times."3

There were more mining disasters:

•Michel, January 9, 1904: 7 men died in a gas blast.

•Coleman, 1907: 3 men died in an explosion of afterdamp.

•Bellevue, December 9, 1910: 30 men died in an explosion.

•Michel, August 1916: 12 men died in an explosion at the height of a thunderstorm; lightning was discounted as a factor.4

•Coal Creek, April 1917: 34 men died.

•Hillcrest, September 1926: 2 men died in an evening-shift explosion.

•Coleman, November 1926: 10 men died in an evening-shift explosion.

•Michel, July 1938: 3 maintenance men died in an explosion during a thunderstorm.

The 1914 team that performed the inquiry into the 1914 Hillcrest Mine tragedy.

Disaster at Hillcrest

The worst mining accident occurred in 1914, when Canada's deadliest mine disaster horrified the Pass and the world.

The Hillcrest mine had an enviable reputation as a safe, well-run mine. Idle for two days because of over-production, the mine opened as usual on June 19, 1914. Of the 370 or so men who reported for work, 235 headed underground. Only 46 of them would see daylight again.

At about 9:30 am, a massive explosion rocked the mine site. At each of the two entrance tunnels that led to the mine, the rope-rider—who unhooked coal cars brought up by cable and shunted them to a tipple—was killed by a great blast of air, which, seemingly out of nowhere, hurtled out from the tunnels below. The blast was strong enough to level a 20 centimetre thick concrete wall in the hoist house.

Initially, some outside workers tried to locate and help survivors below, but they were forced back by clouds of deadly black damp (carbon dioxide). Remarkably, even miraculously, over a dozen survivors stumbled out of the one entrance tunnel that was still functioning.

Within a half hour of the blast, an emergency hospital had been set up at the entranceway; oxygen masks had arrived from Blairmore; a doctor had come; a special mine rescue car had arrived from Coleman. Many miners were also on their way to help out.

The extent of the tragedy soon became clear. Teams returned with body after body. The explosion itself or clouds of gas and dust had taken the lives of most of the men working underground, but throughout the maze of tunnels were some survivors. Many men had temporarily protected themselves by wetting their shirts in pools of water, then breathing through the cloth to filter out gas and dust.

No easy answers could be found regarding cause and blame. No single explanation was advanced that all people would accept.

During the early hours of June 19, before the men had reported for work, a fire-boss had routinely checked out conditions in the mine and pronounced things safe. Although he had encountered several small rockfalls and a few pockets of methane gas, such conditions were to be expected as a matter of course. Moreover, a three-man committee from the mine-workers' union had also checked the mine and declared it safe.

At first, it was suspected that the fire-boss, or "powder man," for the day, Sam Charlton, was responsible for the explosion. Rescuers discovered, however, that although he had set charges at the coal face he had not yet hooked up the wiring and connected the battery before the great blast occurred.

Harry White, a former Hillcrest fire-boss, was the first man to thoroughly investigate the mine soon after the blast. In the minds of many people, his explanation rang true. White believed that a rockfall had produced a spark that ignited a pocket of methane gas and, subsequently, a flame jumped from pocket to pocket of methane until it hit a concentration of coal dust near the coal face. (At a particular state of dryness and concentration, coal dust is as dangerous as gunpowder.) The explosion, White maintained, occurred at the moment of contact between flame and coal dust.

On June 21, a mass funeral for 150 men was held at the Hillcrest cemetery. Undoubtedly, it was the saddest day ever experienced in the Crowsnest Pass. About 400 children had lost fathers, and about 130 women had been widowed.

At the time the world's third worst mine disaster, the Hillcrest mine disaster has remained Canada's worst.

Chapter 7

The Pittsburgh of Western Canada

The Crowsnest Pass area has long been one of the greatest coal-producing areas in Canada. Easily obtainable coal reserves in the area are estimated to be about 5.4 billion tonnes. In the past, as much as 2.7 million tonnes have been extracted from the Pass's mines. Each side of the Pass has served as its province's leading producer of coal. Not surprisingly, coal and the establishment and growth of towns have been synonymous in the Crowsnest Pass.

Crowsnest Pass coal is a medium-volatile bituminous coal, and much of it is excellent for both steaming and coking. Situated in very large bands that are perpendicular to the Pass, the coal seams become thicker and more numerous to the west and south.

Pass coal would not have been mined commercially were it not for the building of the railway through the Pass in the late 1890s. The railway permitted access to the hardrock smelters of eastern British Columbia and the northwestern United States. Moreover, the railway itself created a very important market for local mines: for many years, the single most important customer for Pass coal was the CPR, whose steam engines required a large amount of coal.

British Columbia Coal Mining

Soon after railway construction began, the Crow's Nest Pass Coal Company began mining operations close to Fernie at Coal Creek, BC. The general manager of the company, William Blakemore, brought about 20 Welsh miners from Nova Scotia in December 1897. By the time the CPR reached Coal Creek in August 1898, these miners had dug 1200 metres of underground tunnels and excavated 9000 tonnes of coal. Production reached 320 to 360 tonnes daily by 1899, by which time 50 coke ovens existed. Average daily production stood at 900 to 1450 tonnes by 1901, and 360 coke ovens were operating. One observer stated that "the amount of work accomplished almost surpasses belief."[1]

Completion of the railway marked the beginning of a long period of great success on the part of the Crow's Nest Pass Coal Company, which owned virtually all the coal measures on the BC side of the Pass. Because of its central location and ideal townsite, Fernie was chosen for the company's headquarters. In 1898, mining began at Michel.

Left: With little more than a pick, a shovel, and a helmet, men were required to work long hours, often under deplorable conditions, to mine Crowsnest Pass coal.

Coke ovens, like this one at Fernie in 1899, could hold up to 45 tonnes of coal each and produce up to 3.6 tonnes of coke.

The CPR had one mine on the BC side of the Pass. In 1908, in accordance with the federal government's grant provisions, the CPR chose the area where it would mine. The granted area became known as Hosmer, and the company began mining there almost immediately. The Pacific Coal Company, a CPR subsidiary, installed an elaborate cleaning system for coal and set up 240 beehive ovens for making coke. The company also built some excellent cottages; soon, many hopeful miners arrived at the town.

Hosmer boasted three hotels, a bank, a Methodist church, an opera house, a two-room school for 73 pupils, housing for residents, a board of trade, and a volunteer fire brigade by 1910. To be sure, things looked promising. But, then again, in the Pass, uncertainty reigned supreme when it came to assessing both the local coal industry and towns.

Hosmer, a town which was growing so auspiciously, was destined for a severe and rapid end. As one writer has noted, "In June, 1914, the Canadian Pacific Railway found that their property [here] was unprofitable through dirty coal of poor quality and characteristically closed the mine without delay."[2]

Construction of mine and tipple, Bellevue, ca. 1903. West Canadian Collieries, the company which owned this mine, played a significant role in the economy of the Pass until it closed in 1957.

Alberta Coal Mining

Because of the dominance of one strong company in British Columbia, entrepreneurs and investors looked to the Alberta side of the Crowsnest Pass, where the development of coal was open to all.

Many factors accounted for the rapid rise of coal mining on the Alberta side. Of these, the most determining factor was the state of the Canadian economy. A host of mines appeared and disappeared. All such enthusiastic commercial activity was predicated on a booming assessment of the economy as a whole.

Shortly after the turn of the century, "the world depression had passed and the prospects for industrial and commercial development across Canada looked very good indeed. A new optimism took hold of the nation, its politicians, and its businessmen. The future seemed limitless."[3] In such an environment many investors and developers were eager to spend money. The coal developers of the Crowsnest Pass envisioned a successful local iron and steel industry along with the thriving smelting operations of the area, making the Pass the "Pittsburgh of western Canada."

Miners at the mine entrance of West Canadian Collieries at Bellevue, 1905.

The founders of mining companies active in Alberta at this time were a special breed. Before their arrival on the scene, most of them had acquired a great deal of business experience in British Columbia and in the northwestern United States. Individualists one and all, they believed that people possessed the ability to advance their financial status through prudent risk and considerable effort.

As construction of the railway proceeded, throngs of prospectors inundated the Pass, looking for mineral wealth. The seams are of short fault formation, and they outcrop for kilometres to the north and south; the distances between the various outcrops are only two kilometres or so. Various prospectors, then, made discoveries along the same seam. At Coleman, for example, three separate mine operations were established along the same seam. This state of affairs at first led to a large number of mines and townsites. Only properties with easy access to the railway, however, developed into significant mines.

By 1910, at least 12 companies had begun mining. Around these mines, 10 communities were established: Frank, Coleman, Bellevue, Hillcrest, Blairmore, Lille, Burmis, Passburg, Lundbreck, and Beaver Mines. Only the first five towns have survived; the others disappeared when the local mines were shut down.

Like Hosmer, BC, Lille, Alberta, is an example of the precarious state of Pass towns up to the 1920s. At the local mine, production began in the fall of 1903. Fifty Bernard coke

West Canadian Collieries employed many of Bellevue's men during its long presence in the Crowsnest Pass. In this photo of 1905, the wooden shack behind these workers served as a powerhouse, blacksmith shop, and mine entrance.

ovens were installed. Houses appeared, and a school with 30 pupils was opened. A roomy hotel was erected, as was a 15-bed hospital. Daily production was 635 tonnes of coal by 1907. A tipple was installed, and a wet washer was used to clean coal intended for the ovens. All seemed well.

A few years later, the Lille mine ran into difficulties. In a number of pockets, coal appeared that was dirty. With operation costs high and the coke market poor, West Canadian Collieries decided to close the mine; by 1913, it was abandoned.

Clearly, Pass towns could become doomed, virtually overnight. Small wonder it was that, over the years, Pass residents could never exhaust their curiosity about business matters relating to mining and financing. Often, rumours spread rapidly, and people avidly sought to find out if there was any truth to them. As a result, insecurity in general was part and parcel of Pass life.

Problems in the Pass

During 1912, unemployment was a problem in the Pass. Closing of the Lille mine worsened things. Moreover, the closing of the mine was the first real setback that the Pass had received.

By 1909, 12 mining companies had been established on the Alberta side of the Crowsnest Pass. When the boom ended in 1913, the coal market could not continue to support all these coal companies, and a number of them were forced to close shop. By 1915, 6 of the 10 communities established around the Alberta mines were struggling to survive, or had disappeared. After 1915, only 5 of the 12 companies on the Alberta side were still in operation.

Nonetheless, there were specific factors at play that also affected the ability of coal companies to survive. One perennial problem was that coal mining was an expensive undertaking, and financial difficulties were common for companies. In addition, the unique geology of the Pass meant that important operational problems had to be handled: "The coal seams of the region proved difficult and at times dangerous to mine. They lay at steeply pitched angles, did not generally follow continuous paths, and contained lethal pockets of methane gas. [These] circumstances…added to the cost of day to day operations."[4] Moreover, the "steep pitch of the seams meant that labour-saving machinery was too heavy to be held at an angle against the coal face. Consequently, underground operations in the Pass were labour intensive and more costly than in many other mines."[5]

Other problems were encountered by companies: miner-management relations were poor; coal markets fluctuated; railway car shortages caused transportation problems; the quality of coal seams was unpredictable; accidents could halt operations; breakdowns occurred in the haulage system and at the processing plant. All of these factors affected the companies' ability to compete for and to retain and expand markets.

With the development of new fuels and the onset of the Great Depression, changes needed to be made. In 1935, two of the five surviving companies in Alberta joined forces; two others did the same in 1939. Then, in 1952, with increasingly tight markets, those two amalgamated companies merged to form Coleman Collieries. In 1957, West Canadian Collieries failed, and in 1983—with the loss of Japanese markets—Coleman Collieries failed. The coal-mining era on the Alberta side of the Pass came to an end.

On the BC side of the Pass, the Crow's Nest Pass Coal Company was bought out by Westar Mining; the latter went into receivership in the 1990s. A Calgary-based company, Fording Coal Company, bought the Greenhills mine near Sparwood, BC. Currently, it is upgrading the mine at a cost of $2 million. Although the company can now only keep one-quarter of the workers on the payroll, the mine should be fully reopened in 1995.

In the 1960s, large-scale coal mining came to the Sparwood area with the opening of five major open-pit coal mines. These mines employ over 3000 people and utilize state-of-the-art technology. Reclamation programs are considered among the best in the industry, exceeding government regulations.

Unions

Underground coal miners have always had to anticipate the possibility of injury and death in the course of everyday work. Safe working conditions have been a primary demand of miners over the years, but their voice has not always been heard. Concerted pressure by miners' unions has often been the only means of ensuring this end.

Aside from worker safety, a wide variety of concerns impelled miners of years past to organize unions. One such concern was the use of child labour (above-ground) at Alberta mines until 1914. Other grievances included low pay, unjust treatment by pit-bosses and other company authorities, and the unsanitary conditions that prevailed at company-owned lodgings.

Mine tunnel interior with tracks for coal cars, ca. 1915. This view of a coal mine helps to convey the solitude of the miner, working far underground.

These and other issues prompted coal miners of the early decades of this century to take their place in the vanguard of Alberta's trade union movement. Their resoluteness and militancy were amply displayed on many occasions.

The first miners' unions in Alberta were founded in the late 1890s and early 1900s at Lethbridge and in the Crowsnest Pass. By 1906, most miners in Alberta—some 2200 strong—were members of the United Mine Workers of America (UMW), an affiliate of the American Federation of Labor.

The first miners' strike in the province seems to have been one in Lethbridge in 1897. In 1905, that city was the site of another such strike, but one that turned violent.

Interior of tipple, West Canadian Collieries, Bellevue or Blairmore, 1950s.

Ten days after the strike began, a detachment of mounted police arrived to prevent any damage to mine property and to safeguard strikebreakers. Mounties in the West would do likewise many times in coming years.

In the early 1920s, the coal industry entered an extended period of general decline. To prop up falling profits, Alberta mine operators cut wages and locked out those who would not accept rates of pay below that set by the UMW.

The Alberta UMW collapsed in 1925. By the end of the year, the new Mine Workers' Union of Canada (MWUC) was founded in the Pass; its members were the miners of Blairmore, Bellevue, and Coleman. It was a contradictory amalgam of moderates and left-wingers (most of these were Communist-led).

In 1930, Canadian Communists formed the Workers' Unity League, a trade union centre dedicated to tough bargaining and progressive stands. By 1931, left-wingers in the MWUC were in the ascendancy, and the union accordingly joined the militant Workers' Unity League.

These events coincided with increasingly grim socioeconomic conditions in the towns of the Crowsnest Pass. The coal crisis resulted in men being seriously underemployed. One or two days' work per week was about all any miner could expect, and this situation persisted for years. Inadequate food supplies compounded the difficulties facing

For several decades—into the 1920s—horses were used to haul coal in rail cars.

Small steam engines, or dinkies, started hauling coal in Pass mines beginning in 1920.

Two miners examining tunnel supports, 1941. The sides and roofs of tunnels had to be properly buttressed for safety.

miners and their families.

Miners' grievances against their employers began to build. Especially maddening was the favouritism in evidence. Pit-bosses often chose miners they particularly liked for a day's work and overlooked those with far greater seniority. The introduction of new machinery was also deeply resented.

Early in 1932, a rumour of coming wage cuts spread. Suppressed militancy surfaced throughout the Pass. On February 23, following a minor incident, the Blairmore miners went on strike. The next day, Bellevue miners joined them. A few weeks later, those at Coleman did the same.

The strike was very well-organized and lasted until Labour Day. The 850 strikers were determined to end discriminatory practices regarding the allocation of work. The employers, for their part, sought to break the miners' union, the MWUC. The result was essentially a draw.

Chapter 8
Life in the Pass

*T*he period of expansion in the Crowsnest Pass ended in about 1911 with the proliferation of smelters in British Columbia. As smelters in the province were closed down, so were nearly all the coke oven batteries in the Pass. Despite the increasingly difficult economic situation, however, a land boom on the Alberta side lasted from 1910 into 1912.

Early Developments

The rugged and rough life of people of the Pass was especially pronounced during the frontier era, which lasted until 1916. With most of the population consisting of young, unmarried men, alcohol abuse had become a problem as early as 1899. By 1904, there were 10 hotels in operation. Breweries were established at Fernie, Morrissey, and

Barroom at the Blairmore Hotel, early 1900s. Burdened by long hours of physical labour in the mines, and isolated from other communities by the mountains, miners often searched for solace and companionship in the barrooms of the Pass.

Blairmore Canadian Legion hockey team, provincial Junior hockey champions, 1928. Several players went on to join teams at the professional level. Sports of all types played an important role in the social life of the Pass.

Blairmore.

Prohibition was very unpopular in the Pass, and along with drinking came lawlessness. Crime was prevalent enough that bank messengers were armed, and sometimes retained a police escort. The staff of banks regularly engaged in target practice.

Difficult living conditions remained a problem for many years. Generally, housing throughout the district was poor from the outset. Houses were made of wood; many rested on blocks, which made them easy to move when mines were closed. The closest thing to plumbing, in most cases, was the outdoor privy. After Fernie's disastrous fire of 1908, this town became the only exception. Fireproof buildings were required by law, and a sewer system was also in operation.

One day during this early period, a miner in West Coleman invited some friends for dinner at his shack. Back then, miners kept care of their own dynamite for blasting; if it became wet, it would be useless, so it was usually kept in the oven. As the guests entered the residence, a great explosion literally blew them out of the house. The host had started his fire, forgetting about the dynamite. Remarkably, no one was seriously injured.

In Pass towns, hotel fires were a frequent occurrence. And, often, such fires would also

Interest in music began at a young age in the Crowsnest towns, as seen in this photo of a children's orchestra in 1927.

Music has always played a significant role in the community life of the Pass, with many towns boasting their own band, such as the West Canadian Collieries Band of Bellevue and Blairmore shown here in 1939.

The population of the Pass is composed of many ethnic groups, such as the Bukovians featured here in traditional dress.

burn to the ground whole blocks of houses. Fire-conscious townsfolk set up fire brigades as a result, and, early on, firehalls appeared in newly established towns. Firemen's sports days were extremely well-attended, the main events of the day being hose-laying races and ladder climbing. Money from the firemen's ball, also popular, went toward purchasing hoses and carts.

Miners engaged a good deal in bowling, pool, and other games. Plenty of gambling occurred in conjunction with these endeavours. From the outset, hockey, soccer, and baseball were enjoyed by large numbers of enthusiastic Pass residents. The first hockey game was played in January 1901, in Fernie, between two local teams. Leagues were formed, and championships were up for grabs. Skating rinks made an early appearance, the first covered rink having been established at Fernie by 1908. At it, famous women's hockey teams played for some years. All towns had at least one open-air rink by 1910.

In the early 1920s, hockey received a real boost in the Pass. In 1922 and 1923, large indoor ice arenas were built at Bellevue, Blairmore, and Coleman. Several times, Pass teams won provincial and western championships. Many players went on to become major league players.

Curling began about 1910, and soon had a wide following. Horse racing was well-

Ukrainians in traditional dress. Many Ukrainians settled in the Pass during the early part of this century.

supported, and each town had its own racetrack. Local boxing matches drew big crowds for some years.

Many people in the Pass were involved with groups such as lodges and churches. Particularly active lodges were the Oddfellows, Masons, Knights of Pythias, and Eagles. They held fancy dress balls and masquerades. Local churches had organizations and would often hold church suppers for the community. Automobiles and movies began to appear in goodly numbers during the 1920s, dramatically altering the nature of leisure-time activities.

Music has long been an integral component of community life in the Crowsnest Pass, with many children having learned to play one instrument or another. Bands have been a common feature of towns. A number of "opera houses" were built in the Pass, and, at these, travelling shows performed. The annual March Blairmore Lions Music Festival dates back to 1926. The purpose of the week-long festival is to evaluate speech, choral, and instrumental arts. Adjudicators, who are often professional musicians or teachers, judge the over 300 entrants. The Crowsnest Pass Symphony Orchestra was founded in 1926 (as a string orchestra) and is the oldest amateur symphony orchestra in Alberta. The group's objectives are to train young musicians and to provide music for recreation.

World War I had a significant impact on the Crowsnest Pass. Since most residents were of British, French, or Belgian origin, many volunteers served in the armed forces.

First complete workers' administration, Blairmore, 1934. Harvey Murphy, seated on the far left of the front row, did much to radicalize miners during the 1930s.

Many central Europeans also lived in the Pass, and many of them were arrested and interned. In the Fernie-Michel area alone, 306 people were rounded up. As elsewhere in Canada, residents participated in Red Cross drives, knitting, sewing, and raising money for war charities.

The Great Depression and World War II

Severe unemployment in the Pass led to the radicalization of most workers and of the trade union movement, and this had an effect on Pass politics. The major figure of radicalism was an organizer named Harvey Murphy. He was able to gain a paramount role in the unions, which, since the mid-1920s, had been largely local wage-bargaining entities. Accordingly, the Mine Workers' Union of Canada was replaced by Murphy's Workers' Unity League.

In politics, "workers" slates were advanced, and many aspirants were elected to school boards and town councils. In Blairmore, the new workers' council changed the name of the main street from Victoria Street to Tim Buck Boulevard, after the imprisoned national secretary of the Communist party. Two electric signs advertised the road's name. This action earned Blairmore national attention, virtually all of it sensationalistic and condemnatory. In time, the name was dropped.

On propitious occasions, mass meetings and demonstrations of solidarity were held. Parades, complete with large banners, were held from time to time. Frequently, 24-hour protest or sympathy strikes were held. The determination of workers was expressed best in the 1932 protest; election of the Blairmore workers' town council was one result of this strike.

The Workers' Unity League was disbanded in 1936 and, acting on the recommendation of Harvey Murphy, miners voted to join the United Mine Workers of America. The Mine Workers' Union of Canada passed out of existence.

Fernie was hit hard by the Great Depression. The Coal Creek mines only worked 77 days in 1932, 90 in 1933, and an average of 150 days over the next three years. In August 1932, the salaries of city employees were lowered as a cost-saving measure; at that time, the mayor stated that all relief work would end because of lack of funds. Some time later, the BC government came to the assistance of the suffering city.

The federal government established work camps, and some major projects were undertaken. An emergency landing field for airplanes was built west of Coleman. Camps near Michel, Fernie, and Elko housed men who worked on roads. Men at camps in Bellevue and Frank built a road through the Frank Slide. Men received board, clothing, and 20¢ a day. The camps remained until the mining industry could support the workers once again.

In 1932, coke manufacturing began in a few ovens at Coleman. By the following year, a full battery of ovens operated to supply a smelter at Trail, BC. Because of this, Coleman was the first town in the Pass to recover from the early stages of the Depression. As the overall market improved, and as the market for base metals expanded—and, hence, the market for coke—the economic situation of other Pass towns improved considerably.

During World War II, the demand for coal increased. The mines functioned on a more regular basis, and wages rose; the work week was reduced to five days. The demand for coal rose dramatically. Eventually, because of the National Resources Mobilization Act, no miners were called up. Many men returned from the services on special miners' leaves.

Nevertheless, a substantial number of Pass men signed up to serve during the war; many of them served as engineers. Back at home, the bond drives were well organized and always oversubscribed.

Approaches: Fort Macleod and Cranbrook

As explained in chapter 4, from 1874 until the early 1880s, Fort Macleod was the most important settlement in southern Alberta. Despite a serious setback—with the building of the CPR and the rise of Calgary—by the early part of the new century, the town's fortunes improved: it became an important railway junction, being a major stop along the Crow's Nest Railway and a terminus of the Calgary-Macleod line. Continuing to function as a regional distribution point for a very large ranching/farming area, the town also became a judicial seat. Some notable trials were held there, such as that of the Blood Native, Charcoal, who was hung in 1897 for the murder of a NWMP sergeant.

One interesting custom at the town was the Treaty Tea Party. Until World War I, it occurred on Treaty Day, which came twice a year: in April and October. On these days, Natives from two nearby reserves, Blood and Peigan, received their federal treaty payments. Natives made their way to town with ponies, wagons, carts, and children. Local stores, hoping to bring in a little extra cash, ordered extra stock for the occasion.

While in town, the Natives camped by the river. The highlight of their stay came when a huge tea cauldron was set up behind the Hudson's Bay Company store. The Natives attended the resulting tea-drinking. Children were given fistfuls of hard-coloured candy, while their elders drank the excellent, special tea.

By 1924, Macleod had long been just a minor Mounted Police post, and the old historic fort had closed two years before. However, it had become one of the largest and most prosperous Alberta towns, boasting modern improvements and excellent businesses, and serving as a central point for tourist traffic.

During the Great Depression of the Thirties, the town and area suffered from unemployment, drought, and falling farm prices. Things improved somewhat by the end of the decade, then, in 1940, a training school for pilots was established at Macleod, and the wartime military revenues expended brought the town fully out of depression conditions. Throughout the Forties, much commercial and residential building occurred, highways were improved, and tourism increased. During the Fifties, the population continued to steadily increase, commerce was brisk, and the citizenry demonstrated a considerable—and, as it proved, continuing—interest in education, sports (including figure skating, hockey, and swimming), and cultural activities.

From the Sixties to the present, Fort Macleod has continued its dedication to promoting education, sports, and culture. Fine schools have opened, and, in 1974, the RCMP Centennial Library was opened, for example. The Midnight Stadium was built in 1966, and an excellent arena opened in 1987. In 1972, the Fort Macleod and District Recreation Board was formed to provide greater recreational opportunities in the area. In 1981, the town bought 82 acres for recreational purposes. In 1959, a replica of historic

Fort Macleod was completed. In the early Eighties, historic preservation of downtown commercial buildings began. In 1984, the downtown was designated a Provincial Historic Area, and, since then, many buildings have been restored, renovated, or rehabilitated. (Background: see next section.) Partly due to this, tourism thrives locally, and over 70,000 tourists arrive annually. In 1994, Fort Macleod had a population of 3,112 people.

In 1885, Colonel James Baker bought the grazing lands known as Joseph's Prairie, which had originally been bought from the Upper Kootenay Natives by entrepreneur John Galbraith for $30. The latter also sold Baker thousands of acres of surrounding land he owned. In 1897—because the upcoming CPR's Crow's Nest Railway would cross his lands—Baker had a survey made, set up a land office, and, once the railway arrived, sold lots.

Named Cranbrook, the town expanded quickly. Lumbering at nearby Lumberton was an impetus for growth, as was cattle raising; likewise, the railway spur line, built in 1900, to the rich mines at Kimberley. In 1903, regional provincial government offices were located in the town, Later, it became a CPR divisional point, and residences, a roundhouse, and shops were located there. Incorporated as a city in 1905, Cranbrook became the first urban centre of the East Kootenays.

The city is very strategically located. Connected by road to Kimberley, it is also, extremely importantly, along the southern British Columbia Highway, extending from Vancouver through the Crowsnest Pass and beyond. Via a highway to Penticton and beyond, it has direct access to the Trans-Canada Highway. Also, via a highway that extends south from the town of Yahk (west of Cranbrook), the city has direct access to and from the United States. Tourism has been greatly assisted by such fine access to this transportation centre and very scenic city and area.

The St. Eugene's Mission Church (just north of the city proper) was built in 1897 with funds from the sale of two mining claims which were discovered by Pierre, a Ktunaxa Kootenay Native. (Restored in 1983, it is the finest Gothic-style mission church in the province and features hand-painted stained glass windows.) A school was built there in 1912 and was the home and educational institute for Native children from the Kootenays and the Okanagan. The school operated for many years.

Because of the railway, local industry was stimulated and the city grew steadily. The expansion and diversification of forest industries helped population figures, too. As elsewhere, the city and area suffered from the Great Depression; the population declined by 500 people from 1931 to 1941, the latter figure standing at 2, 568. Since World War II, the economy grew quite well. Forestry, in addition to business from Kimberley helped the staple income from transportation, industry, and tourism. For decades now, Cranbrook has been firmly entrenched as the major transport and distribution centre of the East Kootenay region.

In Cranbrook's Golden Jubilee Year, 1948, the mayor made a rather revealing reference to what Cranbrook residents were proud of, locally. He referred to their educational institutions, industry, and recreational opportunities. Indeed, the major themes of Cranbrook life centre largely around recreation, education, and cultural concerns (including heritage matters.) From the first and last themes, of course, arise the attractions of the city for the great many tourists who visit the location.

In recreational terms, over 100 crystal-clear lakes are in the general area, and a full 20 parks are within city limits. In addition to a beautiful golf course and tennis courts, there is a 20-acre Recreation Complex, featuring a large indoor-outdoor swimming pool. There are hiking and cycling trails just minutes from the city centre.

The city has a fine network of schools, of which it is very proud. Also, it is home to the East Kootenay Community College. The college offers many credit and non-credit courses, and, in 1992, a $4.1 million expansion was completed. By AD 2000, the college should be double its 1990 size.

In the cultural/heritage area, the Canadian Museum of Rail Travel is a very significant feature of the city. (See Guide chapter herein.) Moreover, on the local side, there is a designated self-guided tour of heritage buildings, close to downtown, easily undertaken on foot or by car. In 1992, the 600-seat Key City Theatre opened in the heart of Cranbrook. It is the most modern such facility between Vancouver and Calgary. The theatre hosts a variety of cultural events, apart from live theatre.

With a 1991 population of 16,447, the city is peopled by individuals who value their hometown's assets, notably in terms of excellent educational opportunities, fine leisure-time activities, and a proud heritage.

Saving the Past

More recently, tourism has become important to the economy of the Crowsnest Pass. The history of the boomtown and forts is being preserved.

In March 1981, the Fort Macleod Town Council requested that the provincial minister of culture declare the downtown area an historic district. With the support of the town, the province, and several foundations (including Heritage Canada), in 1982 the Fort Macleod Heritage District Co-ordinating Committee initiated the Fort Macleod Main Street Project.

For three years, the Main Street Project became actively involved in revitalizing and preserving downtown Fort Macleod. In September 1984, it was officially declared a Provincial Historic Area by the government. A grant program was established to assist the restoration, rehabilitation, and promotion of the area, with its 55 buildings, focusing on the historic period of 1910–20.

Not everything has been considered worth saving. Over the decades, considerable pollution had built up from the coal mines at the twin communities of Michel and Natal. The BC government was highly concerned about the situation, not least because Michel-Natal was at the southeastern entrance to the province. A report stipulated that the area's air, water, and land were so polluted that the population should be relocated. Early in 1966, the federal and provincial governments jointly announced the relocation of Michel-Natal residents. Pollution, the age of the buildings, and very limited economic opportunities were some of the reasons behind this decision.

Despite the objections of many locals, the massive relocation scheme began. Residents who refused to sell their houses had them expropriated. The government's actions were controversial and created much bitterness. Many families did agree to what the government offered and moved 8 kilometres northwest to Sparwood, but many left the area altogether. Over the next few years, hundreds of houses, businesses, and public buildings were bulldozed and burned. By 1977, the last phase of the relocation scheme was completed, and Michel-Natal became a memory.

An exciting and intriguing tourist-related concept has been launched in the Alberta side of the Pass: cultural, natural, and historical features of the region are being developed in an ecomuseum. According to this unique system, the "museum" is not a building, but an entire region. The region is the amalgamated Municipality of Crowsnest Pass, which was formed in 1979 by the joining together of all the Alberta communities of the Pass as a new legal entity.

The Crowsnest Pass Ecomuseum was established in 1986 by the municipal council and interested groups. The broad, general theme of coal mining is the framework that knits the ecomuseum's varied activities into a whole. This encompassing theme, or image, helps bind the area and its resources together. Phased development will provide visitors with a variety of experiences, including mine tours, hands-on activities, and walking tours of all kinds—historic, architectural, archeological, natural, and geological.

The first priority of the museum, the rehabilitation of the Bellevue Mine, has been partially completed. Over 365 metres of tunnel and gangway have been restored. Former miners were hired to help with the project. Scheduled underground tours are available in the summer, with visitors donning miners' helmets, battery packs, and lamps. The museum's second priority, the Coleman Journal Building, has also been restored and is now open to the public. The Coleman Journal was a Pulitzer Prize–winning newspaper and provided news and information from 1920 until 1970. Visitors can view two printing presses (one of these still functions) and learn about newspaper printing in the 1930s.

With the closure of mines in the Pass, the tourism industry has assumed crucial importance to the continued well-being of the region. In this respect, the ecomuseum is playing, and will continue to play, a vital role.

Chapter 9
A Legacy of Legends and Notoriety

The folklore of the Canadian West abounds with fascinating tales of murders, rum-runners, and train robbers. The legends of the Crowsnest Pass in particular have captured the imagination of many.

The Lost Lemon Mine

Reportedly, in about 1870, two prospectors named Lemon and Blackjack left Tobacco Plains, Montana, in the company of other hopeful miners. At this time, a number of prospectors were investigating possibilities in the foothills and along the eastern ranges of the Rockies.

The party in question supposedly set out for the North Saskatchewan River. During the return trip, Lemon and Blackjack left their group and joined a party of Natives who were heading south through the foothills. The two eventually left the Natives behind, as well, and headed toward Tobacco Plains.

Reaching the headwaters of a creek or stream, the men happened across an abundance of gold. That night, or soon thereafter, the men quarrelled bitterly over some dispute concerning their discovery. Lemon then grabbed an axe and killed his partner. Taking what gold had been collected, he made his way to Tobacco Plains. There, he confessed his crime to the resident priest. But this did little to ease Lemon's conscience, and after the murder, he became mentally unstable.

The legend also relates that two Stoneys witnessed the killing. It is disputed whether or not the two were accompanying Lemon and Blackjack. Nonetheless, writers agree that the Stoneys eliminated all trace of the campsite following Lemon's departure. They reported the discovery of gold and the grisly murder to their leader, Chief Jacob Bearspaw. The chief supposedly swore the men to silence about the location of the gold. Some writers maintain that Bearspaw also put a curse on the gold.

The richness of Lemon's gold excited much interest among miners in the Tobacco Plains area. Within a few years, a number of them resolved to locate the mine and persuaded Lemon to guide their way. Sufficiently sane to undertake the task, the prospector led the group here and there in the high country, but he could not find the site of the fabulous discovery. When the gold seekers began threatening him with violence and making accusations, Lemon became raving mad. The expedition headed home, empty-handed.

Some writers maintain that Lemon led subsequent, and equally futile, expeditions. It is also stated that the priest at Tobacco Plains financed several trips in search of the elusive gold diggings. As for Lemon (whose Christian name is variously given as Bill, Joe, or Mark), he supposedly spent his latter years at a brother's ranch, in Texas.

Of those who believe that there may well be such a rich deposit of gold, many single out the upper reaches of the Highwood River (roughly 65 kilometres west of High River and Nanton) as the general area. Hundreds of men have scoured the rugged terrain of the Livingstone-Highwood range in search of the Lemon gold diggings. Others have sought the site as far north as Rocky Mountain House, while some have ventured into Montana's mountains and valleys.

While some people believed that the mine was located in an area adjacent to the Crowsnest Pass, others thought that it might be in, or very close to, the Pass itself. Certainly, many of those who sought to find the mine were outfitted at the Pass or departed from there. To date, all such ventures have failed.

Lafayette French devoted much of his life to searching for the lost Lemon mine. A one-time bison hunter, he arrived in Alberta in the 1870s to trade with the Blackfoot. For years, various believers staked his efforts to locate the find. Ultimately, French himself became part of the lore of the story.

In the winter of 1912–13, a mysterious fire broke out in a cabin he was occupying. Badly burnt, he died a few days later. It is said that he managed to say a few words before dying about having solved the mystery of the lost gold.

If a few Stoneys ever did know the site of the gold, the knowledge has been lost. King Bearspaw, grandson of Jacob, gave up his treaty rights in order to search for the gold and work the claim. A much respected tribal councillor and resident of the High River area, Bearspaw spent some 50 years prospecting for the rich diggings.

Auloff's Gang

The first sensational Prohibition-era crime in the Crowsnest Pass occurred in the summer of 1920, at Sentinel, just on the Alberta side of the boundary with British Columbia.

The initial episode involved a CPR train on the Lethbridge to Cranbrook run. Late in the afternoon of August 2, a man in the passenger coach confronted the conductor with a gun. As the conductor pulled the emergency cord, the armed man fired at him but missed. Two other armed men suddenly appeared and prevented any interference by passengers; they collected all the men's wallets and watches. The three men escaped with about $400. The first robber fired a warning shot once he and his friends were outside, to keep the passengers inside. They then began walking toward Coleman.

It is said that the three criminals believed that the wealthy rum-runner/businessman

George Arkoff, ca. 1920. In company with Tom Bassoff and Aubey Auloff. Arkoff robbed a train near the town of Sentinel. He was killed during a shoot-out with police at Bellevue in August 1920.

A re-enactment of the murder of Constable Evens Bailey, a member of the Alberta Provincial Police, by Tom Bassoff in 1920.

Emilio Picariello was aboard the train as a passenger. If this traditional account is true, they undoubtedly looked forward to departing with a large amount of cash in hand.

The robbers, who had not worn masks, were recognized by several people on the train. Their names were Tom Bassoff, George Arkoff, and Aubey Auloff, and they originated from Russia. A manhunt for the three desperadoes was organized by the Alberta Provincial Police (APP), CPR detectives, and the RCMP.

Soon after the robbery, Auloff crossed alone into the United States. His colleagues remained together, heading from one Pass town to another. Five days later, a Bellevue justice of the peace reported to police that he had spotted the two men in a local restaurant. Three policemen entered the establishment and converged on the pair. Shooting broke out. Two policemen—an RCMP and an APP officer—were killed, as was George Arkoff.

Tom Bassoff fled the scene, wounded in one leg. He crawled into the Frank Slide area and evaded detection the rest of the day. Emerging from a choice hiding spot the next day, Bassoff made his way through a police cordon when mist shrouded the valley. He made his way toward Pincher Creek. Near there, on August 11, he was apprehended. In December of the same year, he was hanged.

Aubey Auloff was arrested three and a half years later in Butte, Montana. Extradited

Bootleggers Aldo Montalbetti and Jack Sartoris, with whisky and beer, Frank, late 1910s. During Prohibition, there was a proliferation of bootleggers throughout the Pass.

to Canada, he was tried and sentenced to life imprisonment. He died of natural causes a short time later.

Emperor Pic

The era of Prohibition formally reached Alberta on July 1, 1916, when beer and liquor with an alcohol content of 2.5 percent were declared illegal. In the next five years, the various holes in the province's legislation were filled. Restrictions were passed. By 1921, for instance, no liquor from outside Alberta could be ordered by mail.

From 1916 into the early 1920s, the Crowsnest Pass "became notorious for lawlessness throughout Canada."[1] Indeed, by 1917, the Pass's newspapers "were full of stories of raids on laundries, cafes and other business places by the police who were looking for bootleg drinking places, perhaps because they were open so late."[2]

Although some entrepreneurs concocted moonshine in backwoods shanties, much Prohibition-era liquor was brought into the Pass. Mountain trails were used by pack-horses. Cars also transported contraband alcohol. In terms of the Pass, Fernie, BC, became the main supply centre for Alberta, as well as a major supplier for the United States, which initiated Prohibition in 1914. (Prohibition came later to British Columbia than to Alberta and the United States.)

In the Crowsnest, professional rum-runners set up operations and used swift cars, such as McLaughlin Buicks, Nashes, Cadillacs, and Hudson Super Sixes. There was much competition amongst organized gangs; frequently, opposing gang members tipped off the police as to where liquor caches were located.

Of the various figures involved in big-time liquor dealing in Alberta and British Columbia, Emilio Picariello (also called Emperor Pic, Mr. Pic, and the Bottle King) was the most colourful and notorious rum-running baron. Since he was a wealthy businessman, it is difficult to ascertain exactly why he engaged in such a dangerous enterprise. Perhaps excitement and peril were the stimuli that prompted his involvement.

Emilio Picariello, ("Emperor Pic"), the notorious rum-running entrepreneur, and family, 1915. Picariello was probably the richest and most audacious liquor baron in Alberta during Prohibition.

Born in Sicily, Picariello emigrated to Canada about 1900. Having married a young Italian woman, he arrived in Fernie in 1911. A very sturdy, amiable man with a ready smile and much business sense, he soon bought a macaroni factory, opened a cigar-making plant, and started an ice cream–making business. Also, by about 1916, he cornered the Crowsnest market for empty beer bottles.

In 1918, Picariello bought the Alberta Hotel in Blairmore and became the Pass agent for a Lethbridge brewery, selling the weak brew permitted by law. About three years later, he moved to Blairmore.

Corporal Steve O. Lawson, Alberta Provincial Police, September 18, 1922 just three days after this photograph was taken, Corporal Lawson was murdered outside the APP barracks at Coleman by Florence and Emperor Pic.

Picariello was a major supplier of bootleggers. Maintaining his Fernie contacts, he originated much of his trade from there. Initially, he utilized Model T Fords, complete with concrete-reinforced bumpers for getting through or around roadblocks. Later he used McLaughlin Buicks—then called Whisky Specials—which were expertly serviced by his own mechanic. At one point, he owned six McLaughlins.

All in all, Picariello ran a top-notch operation, not begrudged by most residents of the Crowsnest Pass area. Adjoining the hotel's basement was a specially-built room just right for storing bootleg. "Vehicles could drive right into the basement and any noise of loading or unloading was effectively muffled by a player piano played at full volume in the beverage room above. Not that Mr. Pic had to try to conceal his activities from the local citizens. Most were aware of his sideline and condoned it…he was also respected for being the most benevolent man in the district."[3]

On one occasion, Picariello was proceeding with a full load of alcohol through Whisky Gap, Montana, into Alberta. His car became thoroughly stuck during a bad rainstorm. At a farmhouse close by, he encountered two APP constables who had taken shelter. Enlisting their assistance to free his car, he waved goodbye, smiled broadly, and went on his way. The two policemen never dreamt that the friendly "farmerish-looking man in the sloppy-blue overalls was the noted 'Emperor Pic.' [They] returned to the house to await the cessation of the storm so that they could resume their vigil for rum-runners."[4]

On September 21, 1922, word reached the APP—via a stool pigeon—that Emperor Pic and some of his men would be transporting, in convoy, a large amount of liquor from Fernie into Alberta. Accordingly, two policemen were dispatched to Picariello's hotel in

Emilio Picariello in 1922—the year before he was convicted of murder and hung.

Blairmore. While they waited, search warrant in hand, three McLaughlins approached the Alberta Hotel.

Seeing what was in store just ahead of him, the booze baron hit his horn in the lead car, the signal for his son, Steve, to head back across the BC-Alberta border. (Steve was transporting all the alcohol on this occasion). Soon, the Picariellos were furiously heading for the border and safety, the APP hot on their trail. A frustrated sergeant, James Scott, realized that he would probably not be able to pass Emilio's car on the narrow road leading westward, so he stopped and phoned the constable stationed at Coleman to intercept the rum-runners.

Accordingly, Constable Steve Lawson headed to Coleman's main street, which also served as the highway in question. Lawson arrived as young Picariello was zooming down the road. Nearly hit by the careening vehicle, the policeman got off several shots, one of which hit the young man's hand. By this time, Emilio had effectively blocked the highway behind, leading to Coleman, with his Whisky Special. Lawson commandeered a vehicle, but his chase ended almost as soon as it began because of a flat tire. Young Pic soon made his way across the provincial boundary.

Soon, Emilio was told that his son had been shot by Constable Lawson. Assuming that his son was dead, the distraught father, accompanied by a friend, Florence Lassandro, went to Coleman's APP office. A scuffle broke out between Lawson and Picariello. During the struggle, Lassandro evidently panicked and shot Lawson in the back with her gun. Lawson died within a few minutes. Lassandro's overall role in the chase and subsequent actions has never been fully determined.

Emilio Picariello, Florence Lassandro, and the murder weapon were located near Blairmore the following day. The pair were charged, tried, and sentenced to death. In the midst of considerable controversy, the pair were hanged at the Fort Saskatchewan jail in May 1923.

Notoriety and a touch of legend are part of the legacy of the Crowsnest Pass. The wilder days are long past, but to those who are aware of the stories, the Pass will long remain an area of much fascination.

Chapter 10
A Guide for Visitors

The Great Outdoors

Perhaps the biggest attraction of the Crowsnest Pass is the relatively unspoiled wilderness just a few minutes drive from residential and business areas. Wildlife is varied and plentiful, from the tiny squirrel-like pikas (which scurry among the rocks) to the huge mountain moose (which love to wallow in swamps and sloughs). There are also black and grizzly bears.

Anglers can seek rainbow, cutthroat, brook, bull trout, and mountain whitefish, which can be found in most streams and rivers. Birders will enjoy watching mountain bluebirds, gray and Steller's jays, eagles, and hawks. Bikers and hikers can toil up the many trails available.

Most of the wilderness is located in the Bow-Crow forest, crown land supervised by the Alberta Forestry Service. Many campsites and picnic sites are located in the forest. There is a charge for campsite use. Campfire regulations are strictly enforced, because fires can start and spread quickly.

Motorists will find the groomed and graded gravel roads easily negotiable by the family car. Those with off-road vehicles must find out (from the Alberta Forestry Service office in Blairmore) where use of these vehicles is permitted.

Winter offers even more activities. The Blairmore ski hill has night skiing and a licensed ski lodge. The snow does not prevent wilderness access, and there are well-developed snowmobile and cross-country ski trails. (Back-country travellers are advised to find out the location of traplines by contacting the Fish and Wildlife office in Blairmore).

Historical Driving Tours

Three booklets, providing information for driving and walking tours, have been published by the Crowsnest Pass Ecomuseum and the Coal Association of Canada. A map is provided with each tour, and buildings are numbered along with the streets and avenues. A write-up is provided for each building. Keep in mind that many of the buildings and resources mentioned are privately owned and should only be viewed from the road.

One booklet is devoted to Blairmore, one to Coleman, and one to both Bellevue and Hillcrest. Booklets can be obtained from the Crowsnest Pass Ecomuseum office in Blairmore (403-562-8831), or at the Frank Slide Interpretive Centre, or at the Bellevue Mine Information Centre.

Fort Macleod

The attractive town of Fort Macleod is located in a rich farm and ranch setting, a short drive from some of the most spectacular mountain scenery in the Rockies. The combination of vast open prairie, rolling foothills, and snow-capped mountains provides a dramatic setting for the town's history and natural beauty. The Oldman River flows through the town and facilitates many outdoor activities.

The downtown core of Fort Macleod, southern Alberta's oldest settlement, was declared the first provincial Historic Area. It contains some 30 historically and architecturally rich structures, including a variety of wood frame buildings dating from the late 1890s, as well as many brick and sandstone structures from the early 1900s.

The **Empress Theatre** is one building in which residents take great pride. It is one of the oldest operating theatres in Canada, and the oldest in Alberta. A designated historic site, it has been extensively renovated. The Great West Summer Theatre Company presents plays and musicals throughout July and August.

The **Fort Museum** should not be missed. A replica of the old Fort Macleod, it features displays on the mounted police, the Natives of southern Alberta, and the early settlers of Fort Macleod. A special summer attraction is the Fort Museum's Mounted Patrol Musical Ride, which performs four times daily.

Fort Macleod is a lively town and offers the chance to see live theatre, a parade, and/or a Main Street event, such as the farmers' market and street dances. There are also guided walking tours. A special winter feature is the superb Santa Claus Parade.

Tourism has become one of Fort Macleod's largest industries. Information and brochures can be obtained at the Chamber of Commerce (403-553-4955) or the Main Street office (403-553-2500).

Major attractions near the area include the Remington Carriage Collection in Cardston, Head-Smashed-In Buffalo Jump, the Ecomuseum in the Crowsnest Pass, and the Frank Slide Interpretive Centre. The Fort Macleod Chinook Country Tourist Association offers toll-free information for western Canada and the Northwest states at 1-800-661-1222.

Head-Smashed-In Buffalo Jump

For over 10,000 years, the people of the Plains stampeded herds of bison to their deaths at jump sites across the western prairies. Designated a World Heritage Site by UNESCO, Head-Smashed-In is among the largest and best preserved of these jump sites. Alberta Culture's interpretive centre documents the bison-hunting culture of the Plains people from ancient times to the arrival of the Europeans. It offers a cafeteria, film theatre, and guided tours along two kilometres of outdoor trails, many of which are wheelchair-accessible.

Head-Smashed-In Interpretive Centre is located 18 kilometres northwest of Fort Macleod. The $10 million multi-tiered facility is built into the cliff in order to protect the natural surroundings.

There are five levels of exhibits. Level 1, "Napi's World," has display panels that describe the delicate ecology that exists in the area. (Napi is the mythical creator of the world in Blackfoot legends). Level 2, "Napi's People," looks at the rich and complex nature of prehistoric Plains Native society. Level 3, the "Buffalo Hunt," chronicles the hunt in a widely-encompassing manner. Level 4, "Cultures in Contact," examines the beneficial and the disastrous results of the arrival of Europeans and their technology. Level 5 is devoted to the contributions archeology has made in interpreting the site and in preserving it for posterity.

From Victoria Day to Labour Day, the centre is open from 9 am to 8 pm. During the remainder of the year, it is open from 9 am to 5 pm. It is closed every Monday from November to March. For more details, call 403 553-2731 or 403-265-0048.

Burmis

The **Leitch Collieries Provincial Historic Site** was an important pre–World War I colliery. Its ruins were stabilized by Alberta Culture and Multiculturalism. There is a self-guiding trail, as well as interpretive staff. The self-guided walk primarily takes visitors through the workings of a coke operation. Mining processes are also explained in displays, and visitors can cross a boardwalk to view the mine manager's residence, the washer, and the coke ovens. Guided tours are available, and interpretive staff are on site from 9 am to 5 pm. The collieries site is on Highway 3, near Burmis. From May 15 until Labour Day, it is staffed and open from 9 am to 5 pm daily. It is also open the rest of the year but is not staffed during this time.

Bellevue

The **Bellevue Mine**, which opened in 1904 and closed in 1962, has been partially rehabilitated. Over 365 metres of tunnel and gangway have been restored. Guided tours are available in the summer, with visitors donning miners' helmets, battery packs, and lamps. A gift shop operates outside the old mine.

The mine is open from late June to early September, seven days a week, 10 am to 5:30 pm. There are conducted tours every half hour. The mine is very cool, so warm clothing should be worn. To reach the mine, head to the corner of 213 Street and 25 Avenue, and follow the signs that lead down the hill.

There are several points of interest for the tourist on a driving tour of Bellevue. The one most worthy of a visit is the Bellevue Cafe, a designated Provincial Historic Resource, and the site of an infamous shoot-out between train robbers and policemen in 1920.

Hillcrest

Some miners' cottages still survive in Hillcrest, and a drive through the town will help you spot them and gain an impression of the town's original character. For a glimpse into the darker side of the town's past, there is the Hillcrest Cemetery, a designated Provincial Historic Resource containing the remains of men killed in the Hillcrest mining disaster of 1914.

Frank

The provincial government operates the **Frank Slide Interpretive Centre**. Much of the Crowsnest Pass story is told at the centre, which overlooks the Frank Slide's three kilometre stretch of rock and boulders. An award-winning slide presentation is shown in the theatre. It begins with a dramatic re–creation of the Frank Slide, then briefly examines the other Pass towns. The narrator is W.O. Mitchell, with music by Connie Kaldor.

The centre is open year-round. Its hours from May 15 to Labour Day are 9 am to 8 pm. For the rest of the year, its hours are 10 am to 4 pm.

To reach the centre, follow the signs from Frank. The centre is located 1.5 kilometres north of Highway 3.

Blairmore

The Blairmore Courthouse was the first courthouse in Alberta to accommodate both police and court facilities. A large building, it features an overhanging roof with hipped gables, a main facade broken by distinctive parapets, and decorative brick trim and facing around the windows. The handsome structure now houses the **Crowsnest Pass Ecomuseum Trust**.

The **Greenhill Hotel** is a unique structure that has been designated a Provincial Historical Resource. The former main entrance has a neoclassical portico and the entrances on the east and west sides of the building have main-floor porches and second-storey balconies, both with pillars and wood brackets.

Coleman

Allison Creek Brood Trout Station is located four kilometres north of the highway on Allison Creek Road. This station supplies brook, brown, and rainbow trout eggs for the Sam Livingston Fish Hatchery in Calgary, which breeds fingerlings for Alberta lakes stocking programs.

The station is open seven days a week from May 16 to September 9, 10 am to noon and 1 pm to 3:30 pm. From September 10 to May 15, it is open on weekdays only. Group tours (with a minimum of 10 people) can be arranged by calling 403-563-3385.

The **Coleman Journal Building** has been restored by the Crowsnest Pass Ecomuseum Trust and is open to the public. The Coleman Journal operated from 1920 until 1970. Visitors can view two printing presses (one of which is restored and functioning) and learn about newspaper printing in the 1930s. Interpretive panels and staff explain the history of journalism in the Pass.

The building is located at 7711-18 Avenue and is open Wednesday through Sunday from June 26 to September 1. The hours are 10 am to noon and 1 pm to 4 pm.

The **Crowsnest Museum** presents exhibits on mining, logging, early schools, and businesses in the Crowsnest Pass. There is also an outdoor artifact garden. The latest major project, the Fish and Wildlife room, depicts the natural environment in a creative diorama. Another diorama depicts a horse-drawn coal car.

Volunteers are on duty to guide visitors. The museum is open daily in the summer from 10 am to noon and from 1 pm to 4 pm. In winter, it is open weekdays from 10 am to noon and from 1 pm to 4 pm. The museum is located at 7701-18 Avenue.

The **International Coal and Coke Company Ovens**, situated beside the railway tracks in town, once supplied coke to smelters in the northwestern United States and British Columbia. When the demand for iron, steel, and other metals collapsed at the end of World War I, the ovens were closed down. In 1932, 104 ovens were reopened when a contract was made with a smelter in Trail, BC. The ovens operated until 1952.

The first major commercial building in town was built in 1904. The **Coleman Mercantile Company Store** boasts an imposing facade complete with a tower and a five-sided bay window.

Sparwood

The town of Sparwood calls itself the Southeastern Gateway to the British Columbia Rockies. It is located in the heart of British Columbia's southeast coal mining region. Sparwood is a modern community, with full service and shopping facilities and superb indoor and outdoor recreation amenities.

The local Elk River and its tributaries are home to many sport fish, including cutthroat trout and rainbow trout. Wildlife is abundant in the area. Hiking and biking facilities are available. There is a nine-hole golf course. The Michel Creek and Elk River offer an excellent variety of whitewater recreation, and river access is excellent. A community campground is located on Highway 3. There is a local ski hill with night skiing available and groomed cross-country trails.

The local annual celebration, Coal Miner Days, is held each year in June and features a wide range of family activities.

During June through August, Monday to Friday, tours of Canada's largest open-pit coal mine are conducted. Private tours can be arranged for 20 or more persons.

For detailed information, phone the Travel Infocentre at 604-425-2523.

Fernie

The city of Fernie is a prosperous and tranquil community of some 5500 people. It is the largest community in the Crowsnest Pass.

A fine golf course, open to the public, is backed by expansive and spectacular mountain views. Outdoor recreation opportunities, such as boating and fishing, abound in the area set in the sweeping vistas of the BC Rockies.

The Fernie Snow Valley Ski Resort, a family-oriented location, offers fantastic powder snow conditions. It is open from late November or mid-December to mid- or late April. Temperatures are mild, and the average snowpack is over 450 centimetres per year.

The **Fernie and District Historical Museum** is one of Fernie's oldest heritage buildings. It was erected in 1905 and survived the Great Fire of 1908. Its 10 rooms have been developed with a pioneer theme. Displays include replicas of an early Fernie kitchen, a doctor's office, a school-room, a play/sewing room, and a barroom.

A heritage walking tour leaflet is available at the Travel Infocentre. Two places are worth noting:

The **Fernie Court House** is the only chateau-style courthouse in British Columbia. Completed in 1911, the green-roofed building is an example of late Edwardian architecture, with rich panelling and stained glass windows. The courtroom is lit by six lofty stained glass windows. Most of the finishing of the room is in natural coast cedar.

The **Arts Station** was formerly a CPR station. It has been designated a BC Heritage Building. It was constructed in 1908, after the first two stations burnt down. It is the last surviving "first-class" station of its kind. The building has a new foundation, the exterior has been completely restored, and the interior has been fully renovated. It is now home to a restaurant and the Fernie & District Arts Council.

Fort Steele

The essence of the late 1800s and early 1900s is captured in the streets and boardwalks of the 11 hectare (27 acre) townsite of **Fort Steele Heritage Town**. From the ever-popular street dramas portraying living history to the Clydesdale-drawn wagons, one can easily slip back in time to the days of Queen Victoria's reign.

With a daily schedule and a site map in hand, self-guided tours to every corner of the heritage town are possible. A full day can be spent exploring over 60 buildings, 52 of which are originals or reconstructions of originals. Buildings include a dentist's office, a print shop, a bakery, a general store, a tea-room, a restaurant, and residences. The Wildhorse Theatre also presents live, professional theatre entertainment.

The grounds are open year-round from 9:30 am to 5:30 pm. Entertainment is presented from the latter part of June to early September. For more information, call 604-489-3351.

Cranbrook

At Cranbrook, in every direction as far as the eye can see, the horizon meets with majestic mountain tops. A major distribution centre, it is the largest city in southeastern British Columbia.

The city has myriad attractions for both the vacationing family and the outdoor adventurer. Numerous parks and lakes are readily accessible for summertime enjoyment. Hiking and cycling trails are just minutes from the city centre, and they provide visitors with a wide scope of breathtaking scenery and challenging terrain. A lovely 18-hole golf course welcomes visitors.

Cranbrook values its heritage. A tour of 41 heritage buildings, close to downtown, can easily be undertaken on foot or by car. A favourite time to visit Cranbrook is the third weekend in June, when the city celebrates its annual festival, Sam Steele Days.

The **Canadian Museum of Rail Travel** has an exciting display of a train designed and built in Canada which features a deluxe preserved and restored "hotel-on-wheels." Tours of the restored cars of the 1929 Trans-Canada Limited can include tea and light refreshments in the dining car. The baggage car includes interpretive exhibits and a slide show.

The museum is open daily year round.

For more information on the museum, call 604-489-3918. For information on Cranbrook itself, call the Chamber of Commerce at 604-426-5914.

Notes

Introduction

1. B.O.K. Reeves, "Prehistoric Peoples of the Crowsnest Pass," *Crowsnest and Its People* (Blairmore: Crowsnest Pass Historical Society, 1979), 13.

Chapter 2

1. William James Cousins, *A History of the Crow's Nest Pass* (Lethbridge: The Historic Trails Society of Alberta, 1981), 20.
2. Ibid.
3. Ibid.
4. Cousins, 21.
5. Ibid., 22.
6. Ibid.
7. *The Dynamic Crow's Nest Pass*, Frontier Book No. 5 (Aldergrove, BC: Frontier Publishing, 1969), 13.
8. R.F.P. Bowman, *Railways in Southern Alberta*, (Lethbridge: Whoop-Up Country Chapter, Historical Society of Alberta, 1973), 18.

Chapter 3

1. Ed Arrol, "There's More to See in the Pass," *Calgary Herald Magazine*, 24 July 1970.

Chapter 4

1. Heather Pringle, "Boneyard Enigma," *Equinox* March/April 1988, 88.
2. Ibid., 89.
3. Ibid., 99.
4. Charles Malcolm MacInnes, *In the Shadow of the Rockies* (London: Rivingtons, 1930), 97.
5. *Fort Macleod—Our Colourful Past: A History of the Town of Fort Macleod, from 1874 to 1924* (Fort Macleod: Fort Macleod History Book Committee, 1977) 18.

6. MacInnes, 99.
7. *Fort Macleod—Our Colourful Past: A History of the Town of Fort Macleod, from 1874 to 1924* (Fort Macleod: Fort Macleod History Book Committee, 1977), 19.

Chapter 5

1. D.A. MacDonald and Dave Kay, *Come with Me to Yesterday* (Cranbrook: Cranbrook Courier Press, 1967) 40–41.

Chapter 6

1. Cousins, 83.
2. Ibid., 38.
3. Ibid., 85.
4. Ibid., 86.

Chapter 7

1. Lorry Felske, *The Coal Mining Industry in the Crow's Nest Pass*, compiled by Sharon Babaian (Edmonton: Alberta Culture, 1985), 10.
2. Cousins, 53.
3. Felske, 18.
4. Ibid., 15.
5. Ibid., 15–16.

Chapter 9

1. Cousins, 65.
2. Ibid.
3. Harold Fryer, "Prohibition and the Runners of Rum," *Alberta: The Pioneer Years* (Langely, BC: Stagecoach Publishing, 1977), 53–54.
4. Ibid., 54.

Index

The Author

J. Brian Dawson

J. Brian Dawson has an MA in Canadian and Chinese History and began working as a historian and freelance writer in 1977. He has written over 100 published articles on western Canada. His first book, "Moon Cakes in Gold Mountain: From China to the Canadian Plains" (a history of Chinese Canadians in Alberta), was published in 1991. He lives in Calgary with his wife Patricia. In 1994 they started a marketing business and are joint-venturing with individuals in China, Hong Kong, North America, and elsewhere.

Photo Credits

Doug Leighton: front and back cover, frontispiece

Glenbow Archives, Calgary, Alberta: 11 (NA 1947-7), 15 (NA 1391-1), 16 (NA 712-22), 17 (NA 249-1), 21 (NA 1465-11, 22 (NA 1465-18), 23 top (NA 1465-4), 23 bottom (NA 303-190), 25 top (NA 3833-20), 25 bottom (NC 54-4335), 26 top (NA 3903-32), 26 bottom (NA 5088-1), 28 (NA 3903-1), 14 (NC 54-4324), 30 (NC 54-4332), 32 top (B279-A22), 32 bottom (B279-A4), 35 (NA 23-2), 36 (NA 1434-8), 37 (NA 936-9), 38 top (NA 967-39), 38 bottom (NA 1434-6), 39 (NA 1237-5), 41 (NA 1798-14), 42 (NA 1753-27), 43 (NA 1700-4), 44 (NA 1902-1), 45 (NA 943-31), 46 top (NA 2122-1), 46 bottom (NA 1459-16), 47 (NA 2382-2), 48 (NA 2660-2), 49 top (NA 303-183), 49 bottom (NA 1314-18), 52 top (NA 3662-26), 52 bottom (NC 54-2746), 53 (NA 3011-2), 54 (NA 414-2), 55 (NA 672-3), 56 top (NA 672-1), 56 bottom (NA 823-5), 57 (NA 672-2), 58 (NA 629-1), 59 (NA 3965-70), 60 (NA 1767-5), 62 (NC 54-2864), 64 (NA 1465-10), 65 (3903-12), 66 (NA 3903-10), 67 (NA 3903-11), 69 (NC 54-311), 72 (NA 5088-16), 71 top (NA 712-7), 71 bottom (NC 54-523), 72 (NC 54-2932), 73 (NA 3903-28), 74 (NA 4279-11), 75 top (NC 54-1954), 75 bottom (NA 3903-9), 76 (NC 54-2627), 77 (NA 4279-13), 78 (NC 54-1970), 86 (NA 1146-2), 87 (NA 1146-3), 88 (NA 3903-91), 89 (NA 1136-1), 90 (NA 3537-1), 91 (NA 3282-1)

Sooter Studios: 104